SCHOLASTIC

Comprehension-Boosting
CROSSWORDS
FAMOUS AMERICANS

25 Reproducible Nonfiction Passages With Companion Crossword Puzzles
That Reinforce Reading Skills & Teach About Must-Know Americans

Sylvia Charlesworth

New York • Toronto • London • Auckland • Sydney
Mexico City • New Delhi • Hong Kong • Buenos Aires

Teaching
Resources

Dedication

To the "Fabulous Five"—my grandchildren—
Henry, Beckett, Theo, Dash, and Madeleine

Cover design by Ka-Yeon Kim
Interior design by Holly Grundon

ISBN-10: 0-439-56038-1 / ISBN-13: 978-0-439-56038-2

1 2 3 4 5 6 7 8 9 10 40 15 14 13 12 11 10 09 08

CONTENTS

Introduction 4

Susan B. Anthony 8

Neil Armstrong 10

George Washington Carver 12

Roberto Clemente 14

Davy Crockett 16

Frederick Douglass 18

Amelia Earhart 20

Thomas Alva Edison 22

Benjamin Franklin 24

Thomas Jefferson 26

Helen Keller 28

Dr. Martin Luther King, Jr. 30

Meriwether Lewis & William Clark 32

Abraham Lincoln 34

Thurgood Marshall 36

John Muir 38

Rosa Parks 40

Eleanor Roosevelt 42

Theodore Roosevelt 44

Sacagawea 46

Jonas Salk 48

Harriet Tubman 50

George Washington 52

Laura Ingalls Wilder 54

The Wright Brothers 56

Answer Key 58

INTRODUCTION

Welcome to *Comprehension-Boosting Crosswords: Famous Americans!* In this unique resource, you'll find 25 mini-biographies coupled with 25 companion crossword puzzles. The purpose? To build comprehension, boost vocabulary, and give students an opportunity to spend a few meaningful moments with 25 inspiring individuals—individuals that changed the course of American history.

Picking 25 significant Americans to be represented in this book was both easy and hard—easy because everyone (with a few exceptions) does his or her part to make our country great. Teachers, students, parents and caregivers, fire-fighters, soldiers, artists, athletes, explorers, health-care workers, elected officials, writers, builders, dreamers, performers, volunteers, and people from all walks of life contribute to the amazing and magnificent place that is the United States. Our democracy allows us the freedom to be individuals and to seek out our own destinies. In any city or rural area, one could find numerous people working to make their communities (and indeed, the world) better places for us all. Their stories could all appear here. Every one of them is significant.

This realization is also what made the project so hard. From all these folks, how did I decide on the 25 selected for this book? Familiarity was one criterion. I chose people about whom students may already have some awareness. Variety was also a consideration. I wanted representatives from different professions and areas of life. In addition, I felt that selecting people who personified and participated in "real" historical events would encourage students to learn more about these events. Therefore, most of these 25 are connected to important happenings in our country.

With the exception of Neil Armstrong, all the subjects I chose are no longer living, which allowed me some reflection and perspective on their lives. Of course, some of these people would be on everyone's list. How could anyone overlook Washington or Lincoln, for example? But no two lists would be exactly the same. There are simply too many great people to choose from.

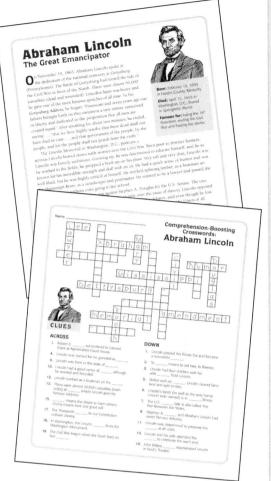

While reading and writing about those who have contributed so much to our country, I realized they had one trait in common: determination. They all listened to their inner voices and acted accordingly. Many began at a very young age to make their dreams come true. These 25 people form a diverse group, but they all have something to show us about what it means to be an American.

I hope your students enjoy completing these crossword puzzles as much as I enjoyed creating them.

Suggestions for Extended Learning

I have arranged the 25 people profiled in this book alphabetically for ease in finding them. One activity that will help students place them in historical context is to create a time line. It could begin with the first European explorations of America and end with the present day. The 25 people written about in this book would be entered in their proper place in time, allowing students to see more clearly exactly where they fit into the story of this country.

As your class reads about these 25 Americans, some will stand out or appeal to different students. You may wish to encourage students to do more reading or prepare in-depth reports about the individuals who particularly interested them or the historical events in which these Americans played a part.

Increasing your students' vocabulary is always a goal. With that in mind, I have selected two challenging words from each biographical sketch that you can introduce to students. (See sidebar on the right.) Because context helps kids learn meaning, I've listed them in the order in which they appear in this book. However, you may wish to alphabetize them and use them for dictionary work instead.

The sky is the limit for the different activities that you can tie to the 25 individuals profiled here. I'm sure you and your class will come up with many original and fun learning experiences.

Featured Vocabulary Words

Susan B. Anthony: suffrage, abolitionist

Neil Armstrong: civilian, lunar

George Washington Carver: inquisitive, tariff

Roberto Clemente: *barrio*, buccaneer

Davy Crockett: legislature, frontier

Frederick Douglass: emancipation, extemporaneous

Amelia Earhart: navigator, kilocycles

Thomas Alva Edison: incandescent, alkaline

Benjamin Franklin: apprenticed, odometer

Thomas Jefferson: endowed, obelisk

Helen Keller: pantomimed, vice versa

Dr. Martin Luther King, Jr.: cadence, orator

Meriwether Lewis & William Clark: expedition, flora and fauna

Abraham Lincoln: malice, dedication

Thurgood Marshall: jurist, unconstitutional

John Muir: mystical, activism

Rosa Parks: plaintiff, segregation

Eleanor Roosevelt: humanitarian, ambassador

Theodore Roosevelt: conservationist, hemisphere

Sacagawea: migrations, interpreter

Jonas Salk: vaccine, poliomyelitis

Harriet Tubman: plantation, manure

George Washington: precedent, persistence

Laura Ingalls Wilder: chronicler, homesteaded

The Wright Brothers: rudder, impeccably

Comprehension-Boosting
CROSSWORDS
FAMOUS AMERICANS

Susan B. Anthony
Fighter for Women's Suffrage

During the 1800s, the life of women was very different from what it is today. By law, women were not allowed to vote in national elections, and therefore could not influence legislation (laws) to further their interests. Their husbands or fathers controlled all household money, even their wages. They were forbidden to own property. Susan B. Anthony, a wage earner herself, and unmarried, felt this inequality keenly.

Very independent, Susan never had the desire to marry. She supported herself for years as a teacher and helped her parents and siblings after her father's business failed. Raised a Quaker, she was tall, thin, conservatively dressed, and rather stern in appearance. But on the inside, she was deeply passionate. A gifted writer, she also traveled frequently, giving speeches and raising money for various causes. But most of her energy was spent trying to obtain the right to vote (suffrage) for women. She felt voting was the key to obtaining other laws to help women. Sometimes in real physical danger, and often mocked and insulted, Susan never gave up.

Born: February 15, 1820, near Adams, Massachusetts

Died: March 13, 1906, in Rochester, New York

Famous for: working very hard to obtain the right to vote for women

She developed a close, lifelong friendship with Elizabeth Cady Stanton, who was also dedicated to women's rights. Stanton's husband, an abolitionist, fought to end slavery. In 1848, Stanton, along with Lucretia Mott and others, organized the first convention for women's rights in Seneca Falls, New York. (The Women's Rights National Historic Park and Hall of Fame there, now commemorate this important event.) Susan B. Anthony had to miss that meeting, but she made up for it later with her hard work and extreme devotion to the cause of women's suffrage. In 1872, she was actually arrested for voting. Tried and convicted, she was fined $100. Till the end of her life, she refused to pay that fine.

One of Susan's many accomplishments was raising $50,000—which was a very large sum of money in those days—so that the University of Rochester would build facilities so it could admit women. She knew that the education of women was an important step toward their full equality. In 1920, 14 years after her death, the Nineteenth Amendment, allowing women the right to vote, was added to our Constitution. Called the Susan B. Anthony Amendment, it passed 100 years after her birth. Shortly before her death, in her last public statement, Susan announced, "Failure is impossible." Thanks in large part to her tireless efforts, she proved to be right.

Comprehension-Boosting Crosswords: Famous Americans © 2008 by Sylvia Charlesworth, Scholastic Teaching Resources

Comprehension-Boosting Crosswords: *Famous Americans* © 2008 by Sylvia Charlesworth, Scholastic Teaching Resources

DOWN

1. Susan B. Anthony worked as a _____ for many years.

3. The word "_____" means the right or privilege to vote.

6. When Susan B. Anthony voted, she was _____.

7. Elizabeth Cady _____ and Susan B. Anthony were fighters for women's rights.

8. Until 100 years after Susan's birth, women were prohibited from _____.

9. Susan's family moved from a farm to _____, New York.

10. Susan B. Anthony's biggest job was to raise _____ to support causes.

11. Susan never paid the $100 _____ she was told to pay for voting illegally.

14. Elizabeth Cady Stanton called a convention to discuss women's _____.

ACROSS

2. Susan was a member of the _____ faith.

4. "_____ is impossible," Anthony said.

5. In 1848 the first women's rights convention was held in Seneca _____, New York.

7. Her father's business failed, so Susan had to help _____ the family.

12. People who wanted to outlaw slavery were called _____.

13. The Women's Rights National _____ Park honors women's fight for suffrage.

15. The _____ Amendment to the U.S. Constitution gave women the vote.

16. Susan raised _____ thousand dollars so the University of Rochester would admit women.

17. A married woman's _____ had control of all household money.

18. _____ Mott joined Elizabeth Cady Stanton in calling the Seneca Falls convention.

19. Susan B. Anthony was born in 1820 near Adams, _____.

Neil Armstrong
Space Pioneer

On May 25, 1961, President John F. Kennedy addressed the Congress of the United States. He said, "I believe that this nation should commit itself to achieving the goal, before this decade is out, of landing a man on the moon and returning him safely to Earth." At that time, there were only seven U.S. astronauts, and 30-year-old Neil Armstrong wasn't one of them. But he was an expert pilot and flew experimental X-15 rocket planes to the very edge of space.

Born: August 5, 1930, in Wapakoneta, Ohio

Famous for: being the first person to set foot on the moon on July 20, 1969

In 1962, the National Aeronautics and Space Administration (NASA) issued a call for a second group of astronauts. This time, Armstrong knew he should be one of them. He applied, was accepted, and became the first civilian (non-military person) in space. Armstrong was a retired Navy pilot. He had won three Air Medals fighting in the Korean War. In addition, he had earned degrees in aeronautical engineering. His first flight into space was aboard *Gemini 8,* which was launched on March 16, 1966. With copilot David Scott, their job was to test space docking (joining two spacecraft as they orbit). The docking was a success, but then the capsule began tumbling wildly, almost killing the pilots. Highly educated, well trained, and quick-thinking, Armstrong saved the craft, which was brought down safely in the ocean.

Neil first fell in love with airplanes after riding in one at the age of six. A Boy Scout and member of the school band, he still spent most of his free time one way or another on airplanes. He built models and read about aviation. He cut grass and worked at a bakery to pay for flying lessons. On his sixteenth birthday, the first thing he did before he even got his driver's license was to earn his pilot's license. In 1969, Armstrong was chosen to command *Apollo 11.* This was the spacecraft that was going to attempt the first lunar (moon) landing.

The rocket launched at 9:32 A.M. on July 16 from Cape Kennedy (now Cape Canaveral) Florida. As more than five million people watched on TV, the *Saturn V* rocket lifted the space capsule from Earth. After one and a half orbits around Earth, the crew of Armstrong, Michael Collins, and Edwin E. "Buzz" Aldrin shot through space on their three-day journey to the moon. When they reached it, they went into orbit. From there they landed the lunar module *Eagle* on the moon's dusty surface. Neil Armstrong stepped outside, wearing a special spacesuit with a portable life-support system (PLSS) on his back. To the entire waiting world, he said, "That's one small step for a man, one giant leap for mankind." And a very big accomplishment for a boy who was born on his grandparents' farm in Ohio.

Name _____

Neil Armstrong

DOWN

1. Neil Armstrong was a Navy pilot during the _____ War.

4. The mission Armstrong commanded to reach the moon was _____ 11.

5. _____ means having to do with the moon.

6. A _____ is a period of ten years.

9. President _____ wanted an American on the moon before ten years passed.

10. "That's one small step for a man, one giant leap for _____," said Neil Armstrong after he stepped on the moon.

13. The name of the lunar module was _____.

14. The *Saturn V* was a _____.

15. As a boy, Neil worked in a _____ to pay for flying lessons.

ACROSS

2. An _____ is the path a human-made satellite or celestial (heavenly) body takes around another body, such as Earth around the sun.

3. An _____ is a person trained to pilot or navigate a spacecraft.

7. Armstrong and David Scott practiced docking on the _____ *8* mission.

8. When spacecraft link up while orbiting in space, it is called _____.

11. _____ stands for National Aeronautics and Space Administration.

12. In 1973, Cape Kennedy went back to its old name of Cape _____.

16. Neil Armstrong's birthplace was _____, Ohio.

17. Armstrong earned two degrees in _____ engineering.

18. Michael Collins, "Buzz" _____, and Neil Armstrong manned *Apollo 11*.

19. On his _____ birthday, Neil earned his pilot's license.

20. After leaving Earth's orbit, it took three _____ to travel the 250,000 miles to reach the moon.

George Washington Carver
Champion Educator

George Washington Carver was born a slave on the farm of a man named Moses Carver. At first, he was known simply as "George." Then people started calling him "Carver's George." He didn't like that, so he took the name George Carver. He added the initial W because there was another George Carver in his school. Someone asked what the W stood for and that's when he decided it stood for "Washington."

Although sickly as a child, George was very intelligent and inquisitive (asked many questions). Early on, he displayed a love and genius for growing plants. Determined to be educated, and with the Carvers' blessing, he walked to the town of Neosho to attend school. There, George was taken in and cared for by a woman he called Aunt Mariah. But he was too advanced for the school in Neosho, and so for the next ten years he wandered about going to various schools and supporting himself doing odd jobs. A talented artist, he eventually studied painting at Simpson College. Many years later, that school awarded him an honorary doctorate degree. Eventually, he ended up a student at the Iowa State College of Agriculture in Ames. But he never lost his love for painting pictures of flowers.

As a young man, Carver vowed he would help poor farmers learn more about the science of agriculture. When Booker T. Washington, the founder of Tuskegee Institute in Alabama, called and asked him to join the faculty there, he agreed. Tuskegee was created to teach African-American men practical skills they could use to earn a living. Carver, a religious man, felt called to help his people.

Cotton had been the king of crops on farms in the South. This constant replanting resulted in seriously depleted soil. Carver introduced the idea of planting a variety of crops, such as soybeans, sweet potatoes, and his favorite, peanuts (from which he developed over 300 products). He wrote and distributed pamphlets encouraging growers to rotate crops and fertilize their fields to keep their soil rich.

A highlight of Carver's life was addressing the U.S. Congress to persuade it to enact a tariff (tax) to protect homegrown peanuts. Because of the importance of his work, he had many influential friends, such as automaker Henry Ford and U.S. Secretary of Agriculture James Wilson. Today, 18 schools and a museum bear George Washington Carver's name. In 1937, a bust of Carver was unveiled at Tuskegee, honoring his 40 years there. At the ceremony, he wore the suit that his classmates had bought for him when he was the first African-American man to graduate from Iowa State College. In his lapel, he sported a favorite flower.

Born: probably July 12, 1864, in Diamond, Missouri (during the U.S. Civil War)

Died: January 5, 1943, in Tuskegee, Alabama

Famous for: promoting agricultural education and research

Name _____

DOWN

1. _____ T. Washington founded Tuskegee Institute.

2. Automaker Henry _____ was a friend of George Washington Carver.

3. One of our U.S. presidents, Jimmy _____, was a peanut farmer.

4. _____ College awarded Carver an honorary doctor of science degree.

5. Carver wanted to use the science of _____ to better the lot of farmers.

6. George Washington Carver invented 300 products made from _____.

8. Many _____ and a museum are named for George Washington Carver.

11. As a boy, George showed a genius for _____ plants.

12. Cotton was _____ in the South, but it made the soil poor for farming.

13. When he was honored at Tuskegee, Carver wore a flower in the _____ of his suit coat.

14. George Washington Carver was born on the farm of Moses _____.

15. When Carver was born, our country was in the middle of the _____ War.

18. George Washington Carver was graduated from Iowa State College of Agriculture in _____.

ACROSS

6. Carver encouraged rotating cotton crops with peanuts, soy beans, and sweet _____.

7. The U.S. _____ listened to Carver's speech about peanuts.

9. A woman Carver called Aunt _____ took him in so he could go to school.

10. _____ Institute is now a university, with over 3,000 students.

16. George's mother was a slave, so that meant George was born a _____.

17. Carver studied _____, but switched to agriculture because it was more practical.

19. As a painter, Carver's favorite subject matter was _____.

Roberto Clemente
Pride of Puerto Rico

"Roberto can hit any pitch, at any time. He will hit pitchouts; he will hit brushback pitches. He will hit high, inside pitches deep to the opposite field, which would be ridiculous even if he didn't do it with both feet off the ground." That's how Dodger pitching great Sandy Koufax, in his autobiography, described Roberto Clemente's astounding hitting ability. Born a "natural," with a fierce desire to play baseball, Roberto was mostly self-taught. He played for hours in his native Puerto Rico, using a guava branch for a bat and knotted-up rags for a ball.

When he was a boy, Roberto and his family were poor. His father cut sugar cane for a living. It was backbreaking work. Every day, Roberto walked half a mile carrying his neighbor's milk jug to the store to be filled. It was very heavy on the trip back, but after three years he had earned and saved $27. That was enough to buy a used bicycle. At a very young age, it was clear he knew what determination was. And Roberto Clemente was determined to play baseball.

Born: August 18, 1934, in Carolina, Puerto Rico

Died: December 31, 1972, in a plane crash into the sea near San Juan, Puerto Rico

Famous for: being the first Hispanic player elected to the Baseball Hall of Fame

One day a scout who was scouring the *barrios* (neighborhoods) for baseball talent spotted Roberto slugging tin cans far out of sight. The scout grabbed him, and for the next two years Roberto played for the Puerto Rican League. Then, in 1954, Clemente was signed by the Brooklyn Dodgers. He was sent to play with the Minor League Montreal Royals, where he spent a very frustrating year. It was cold in Montreal, no one spoke Spanish, he didn't speak French, and he missed his family. The Royals' manager didn't use Roberto much because he didn't want the world to see how good he was. If the Giants saw him, he knew they would try to draft him. But the Pittsburgh Pirates were at the bottom of their league, and got first draft choice. They wanted Clemente and "picked up" Roberto for $4,000. They had a new buccaneer (pirate) in their ranks. They sure got their money's worth!

On September 30, 1972, Clemente slugged his 3,000th hit, putting him in a league with Willie Mays, Hank Aaron, and a few other baseball immortals. Clemente believed in making a difference off the baseball field as well as on. That December, he organized a relief drive for the people of Managua, Nicaragua. The city had been hit by a devastating earthquake, which killed and injured thousands. The loaded airplane, with Clemente aboard, failed soon after take-off from San Juan and plunged into the sea. Everyone was lost. Roberto was immediately inducted into Baseball's Hall of Fame. In 2003, President Bush selected him to receive the Presidential Medal of Freedom posthumously (after his death). Throughout his life, Roberto always wanted to set a good example. And up to the very end, he did.

Comprehension-Boosting Crosswords: Famous Americans © 2008 by Sylvia Charlesworth, Scholastic Teaching Resources

Name _____

DOWN

2. An _____ is the story of your life that you write yourself.

3. As a boy, Roberto used a bat made from a _____ branch.

5. Clemente played for the _____ Royals, but he was homesick.

6. The Pittsburgh Pirates are sometimes called the _____.

9. The Royal's manager was afraid the _____ would spot Clemente and sign him.

11. Roberto's first professional job was with the Puerto Rican Baseball _____.

15. The word _____ in Spanish means a neighborhood where Spanish is spoken.

18. Roberto's father cut sugar _____ for a living.

20. Roberto Clemente was only 38 years _____ when he died.

ACROSS

1. Roberto Clemente was born in _____, Puerto Rico.

4. _____ Rico is a self-governing commonwealth in union with the U.S.

7. _____, Nicaragua, suffered a devastating earthquake in 1972.

8. Dodger pitcher Sandy Koufax said Clemente could hit any _____.

10. The first baseball Roberto used was a bunch of _____ tied together.

12. A "_____" is someone who is born with an amazing ability to do something.

13. Roberto Clemente was the first Hispanic to be inducted into the _____ Hall of Fame.

14. Roberto's plane loaded with supplies for Managua crashed near San _____.

16. Roberto Clemente, Hank Aaron, and Willie _____ had at least 3,000 hits.

17. The word _____ means pertaining to Spain and its people, language, and culture.

19. Clemente was first signed by the Brooklyn _____ but ended up a Pittsburgh Pirate.

Davy Crockett
Legendary Frontiersman

According to legend, David Crockett introduced himself the day he was born and said, "I'm Davy Crockett, fresh from the backwoods. I can ride a streak of lightning and whip my weight in wildcats. I can outfight, outshoot, out-jump any man in the country." He was said to wrestle bears and ride up Niagara Falls on his pet alligator (holding his nose).

We may not believe these "tall tales" about him, but the real Davy Crockett was an extraordinarily brave frontiersman. A popular TV series from the 1950s had a theme song with these words: "Davy, Davy Crockett, king of the wild frontier." The character of Davy was dressed in buckskins (deer hide) and a coonskin (raccoon fur) cap.

Davy was the fifth of nine children born to poor farmers. The family's new mill on Cove Creek washed away in a flood, so they moved and built a tavern for travelers going between Abingdon and Knoxville, Tennessee (TN). When Davy was 12, his father hired him out to a traveling Dutchman. Davy "set out with a heavy heart" for Virginia, but he returned home with new frontier skills and money to help his family. A few years later, when Davy went out to work again, he decided to trade his labor for "book-learning." At age 19, he settled down and married Polly Finley. He used his long-barreled rifle, "Old Betsy," to supply all his neighbors with game (for food). But Davy wasn't the settling-down type, so when General Andrew Jackson asked for volunteers to fight the Creek Indians (1811) Davy volunteered. He was used to facing danger, but when Polly died at age 27, he said losing her was his "hardest trial." He later married a widow, Elizabeth Patton.

Davy Crockett began his political career as a justice of the peace (judge) in Shoal Creek, Tennessee. He said he used "natural-born sense" to decide cases on this rugged frontier. Serving in the Tennessee legislature, he told funny stories, but took the job very seriously. Then he was elected to three terms in the U.S. Congress, but because he often stood up to, and disagreed with, President Jackson, he was voted out in the next election. So he decided to round up volunteers to fight Mexico's General Santa Anna to achieve Texas's independence. On March 6, 1836, Davy was one of 180 men who lost their lives defending the Alamo, a former chapel in San Antonio, Texas. "Remember the Alamo" became the rallying cry, helping Texas win its freedom and eventually become a part of the United States. Davy Crockett was a true hero and soon became a real legend!

Born: August 17, 1786, in Greene County, in eastern Tennessee

Died: March 6, 1836, at the Alamo, San Antonio, Texas

Famous for: being an outstanding frontiersman and defender of the Alamo

Comprehension-Boosting Crosswords: Famous Americans © 2008 by Sylvia Charlesworth, Scholastic Teaching Resources

Name _____

DOWN

1. He was born "David" Crockett, but he was better known as _____.

2. Davy Crockett had a rifle he called "Old _____."

4. More than 180 men lost their lives defending the _____.

5. The _____ is the region beyond a developed or settled area.

6. A tall tale about Davy was that he rode an _____ up Niagara Falls.

7. Andrew Jackson asked for help fighting the _____ Indians.

8. While serving in the U.S. Congress, Davy disagreed with President _____.

9. Davy's "hardest _____" was his wife, Polly's, death.

10. When Davy lost his last election to _____, he went to Texas.

14. Davy Crockett's first political job was justice of the _____.

ACROSS

3. Santa _____ was the leader of the Mexican forces.

6. The Alamo had been the chapel of a mission in San _____, Texas.

11. In the TV show, the actor playing Davy Crockett wore a _____ cap.

12. Davy felt he needed an _____, so he traded his labor for book learning.

13. Davy was elected to the Tennessee _____.

15. When he was 12 years _____, Davy's father hired him out.

16. During the 1950s there was a TV _____ about Davy Crockett.

17. The abbreviation for Davy Crockett's home state is _____.

18. _____ used to be part of Mexico.

19. Davy boasted that he could "whip my weight in _____."

Frederick Douglass
Fighter for Freedom

"We were waiting and listening as for a bolt from the sky . . . we were watching . . . by the dim light of the stars for the dawn of a new day. . . ." Frederick Douglass, former slave, described the feelings of the crowd waiting for word of the Emancipation Proclamation. The Proclamation, issued by President Abraham Lincoln, took effect on January 1, 1863. It was the first step toward outlawing slavery. A former slave, Douglass was a famous abolitionist, but he was also a man President Lincoln called a friend. He was invited to the White House to offer his advice and counsel.

For the first seven years of his life, Frederick, born Frederick Augustus Washington Bailey, lived with his grandparents, while his mother worked in the cornfields. During that terrible time, he witnessed many of the other slaves being beaten. He rarely saw his mother. She had to walk miles to visit him, but when she did, she brought food, comfort, and love. She died when Frederick was 7. Around this time, Frederick moved to Baltimore and lived in the home of Sophia Auld. Frederick wanted to read. Not knowing it was illegal to teach slaves, Sophia taught him. She instructed him to stand tall and look people squarely in the eye. Proud of his success, Sophia asked Frederick to demonstrate his ability for her husband, Hugh. Hugh was frightened and furious and ended the lessons immediately. But a seed had been planted, which grew within Frederick. Determined to be free, he realized education would be the key to his success.

Frederick went back to the plantation where he was born, and worked the fields for several years. Then he was sent back to Baltimore to learn to caulk ships. His wages went to his owner. However, he taught Sunday school and met Anna, a free woman. She helped him escape on a train to New York (with borrowed seaman's papers). Anna lent him money and sewed him a fake sailor's uniform as a disguise. He took the name Douglass to escape being captured and returned to slavery. Frederick and Anna later married up North and had five children.

In 1841, Douglass gave an extemporaneous (unprepared), spellbinding speech at the Massachusetts Antislavery Society. His fame quickly spread. In 1845, he published his autobiography, *Narrative of the Life of Frederick Douglass*. He lived for many years in Rochester, New York, where he published the *North Star,* an influential abolitionist newspaper. His Washington home is now a national monument. A fierce fighter for justice (he also supported rights for women), Frederick Douglass, never bitter, died old, successful, happy, and free.

Born: probably in February 1818, near Easton, Maryland

Died: February 20, 1895, in Anacostia Heights, Washington, D.C.

Famous for: being a gifted speaker, writer, and abolitionist

Comprehension-Boosting Crosswords: Famous Americans © 2008 by Sylvia Charlesworth, Scholastic Teaching Resources

Name _____

Frederick Douglass

DOWN

1. _____ was Frederick Douglass's wife for over 40 years.

2. Frederick Douglass was born near Easton, _____.

3. _____ means unplanned and unrehearsed; off the cuff.

5. Frederick _____ Washington Bailey was Douglass's birth name.

6. Douglass called the Emancipation Proclamation "the _____ of a new day."

9. Frederick was permitted to teach _____ school in Baltimore.

11. _____ Auld taught Frederick to read, be proud, and stand tall.

12. Douglass met with President Abraham _____ at the White House.

14. Frederick took the name _____ so he would escape being captured.

17. Douglass, a friend of Susan B. Anthony, supported rights for _____.

ACROSS

3. When he was very young, Frederick knew that _____ was the key to success.

4. In 1845, Frederick Douglass published his _____.

7. Slaves seeking freedom in the North followed the North _____. The *North Star* was the name of Douglass's abolitionist newspaper.

8. Until he was about 7, Frederick was raised by his _____.

10. People who wanted to abolish (do away with) slavery were _____.

13. It was _____ to teach slaves to read and write.

15. Anna helped Frederick escape by sewing him a sailor's _____.

16. Frederick was taught a trade, which was to _____ ships.

18. Frederick Douglass's home in Washington, D. C., is a national _____.

19. Douglass lived in _____, NY, for many years and he is buried there.

Amelia Earhart
Pioneer Woman Aviator

On July 2, 1937, at 8:44 A.M., radiomen on the Coast Guard cutter *Itasca*, which was a very fast powerboat, received this message: "We are on the line of position one-five-seven dash three-seven-seven. Will repeat this message on 6,210 kilocycles. Wait. Listening on 6,210. We are running north and south." Anchored off Howland Island, a mere speck in the vast Pacific, the *Itasca* was waiting to help guide pilot Amelia Earhart and her navigator Fred Noonan to a safe landing. This was the longest, most difficult leg of Earhart's around-the-world flight, and nearly the last. She had taken off from Lae, New Guinea, with a 2,556- mile journey to Howland Island ahead of her. Her plane, a Lockheed Electra, was noisy and shaky. Traveling for six weeks (including stops), it had carried Earhart and Noonan 22,000 miles. The radio communication above was the last ever received from the aviators. Earhart and Noonan vanished without a trace.

Born: July 24, 1897, in Atchison, Kansas

Died: probably in the Pacific Ocean, July 2, 1937

Famous for: being the first woman aviator to fly solo across the Atlantic Ocean

Amelia (nicknamed Meely) and her sister Muriel (nicknamed Pidge) spent many of their growing-up years with their grandparents, Judge Otis and his wife, also named Amelia. Their father, Edwin Earhart, worked as a claims agent for the railroads and traveled a lot, taking the girls' mother, Amy, with him. The Earhart sisters had happy childhood years and enjoyed a freedom that was unusual for girls at that time. They were encouraged to be physically active and adventurous. As a young woman, Amelia enrolled as a premedical student at Columbia University. While visiting her parents in Los Angeles in 1920, she took her first ride in an airplane. She was instantly hooked on flying, and began her first lessons, working as a social worker to support her ambitions.

In 1928, Earhart was the first woman to cross the Atlantic Ocean by plane. On that flight she was a passenger. But in 1932, she flew on her own across the Atlantic. And in 1935, she soloed from Honolulu, Hawaii, to Oakland, California, and later, from Mexico City to Newark, New Jersey. She broke speed records and set an altitude record in an autogiro (early helicopter). She was a skilled aviator, and her baffling disappearance left many questions unanswered. Was she, as some have wondered, spying for the U.S. and captured by the Japanese as World War II heated up? Or did she simply miss the small island, run out of gas, and drop into the Pacific? The curious are still trying to solve this mystery, but Amelia Earhart's astounding flying records are history. They will never be lost or forgotten.

DOWN

1. At one time Amelia enrolled in premed studies at _____ University.

3. Some people think Amelia Earhart was a spy, captured by the _____.

4. On her round-the-world flight, Fred _____ was Amelia's navigator.

6. Amelia and her sister spent years of their childhood with their _____.

7. _____ Island was Earhart and Noonan's destination when they were lost.

8. Most people think Amelia's plane ditched in the _____ Ocean.

11. For her round-the-world flight, Earhart was flying a Lockheed _____.

12. Noonan and Earhart had already flown 22,000 _____ when they took off for Howland.

13. They took off from Lae, _____ Guinea (a Pacific island).

15. Amelia Earhart was born in Atchison, _____, in 1897.

ACROSS

2. The Earhart sisters enjoyed more _____ than most girls at the time.

5. An _____ was an early airplane something like a helicopter.

9. When Noonan and Earhart disappeared, they had almost no _____.

10. Amelia Earhart flew solo (alone) across the _____ Ocean in 1932.

12. _____ was Amelia's childhood nickname; her sister's was Pidge.

14. In 1937, Amelia Earhart's goal was to fly around the _____.

16. The *Itasca* was a very fast Coast Guard powerboat called a _____.

17. In 1928, Earhart was the first woman _____ to fly across the Atlantic.

18. Amelia was a _____ worker because she liked it and needed money to fly.

19. Radiomen on a boat named _____ received the last message from Amelia Earhart.

Thomas Alva Edison
Tireless Inventor

Thomas Alva Edison was nicknamed the "Wizard of Menlo Park." Menlo Park, New Jersey, was the site of Edison's first major laboratory. He resented that nickname because it implied he used magic to make things work. On the contrary, he said, "Genius is one percent inspiration and ninety-nine percent perspiration." He added, "There is no substitute for hard work." And work he did, often going for days with no sleep and little food. He was so immersed in his inventing, he didn't even notice. Edison was a practical man. He wanted to make things that people could use and enjoy, or improve gadgets already in existence. He held more patents—1,093—than anyone else in the world. (A patent is a grant given to inventors by the government. It allows the inventor the exclusive right to make, use, and sell his or her invention for a specific period.) Edison had 400 patents related to electricity alone. As the inventor of the incandescent lamp (light bulb), he single-handedly ushered in the electrical age.

Born: February 11, 1847, in Milan, Ohio

Died: October 18, 1931, in West Orange, New Jersey

Famous for: beginning the age of electricity

As a child, Edison was curious about everything. Hardworking even then, he raised vegetables. He then sold them to pay for chemicals for his basement laboratory. Because he daydreamed in school and asked too many questions, his mother agreed to teach him at home. Edison once said, "My mother was the making of me." By the age of 12 he had a job as a "candy butcher" on the railroad, selling newspapers and refreshments on trains. During the train's five-hour layover in Detroit, he'd read in the public library. Eventually, he published his own successful newspaper, the *Grand Trunk Herald*. One day, the stationmaster's son was playing on the railroad tracks. An unattended boxcar started rolling toward him. Thomas saw it coming and snatched the boy to safety. In gratitude, the father taught Edison telegraphy. Telegraphy was an early means of communication. Using electrical impulses, a series of dots and dashes called the Morse Code was sent over wires from place to place. Edison worked in that field for years, making improvements on the equipment all the time.

Imagine what your life would be like without electric lights, phonographs, moving pictures, alkaline storage batteries, and telephones. You can thank Edison for all of these luxuries. He also invented the modern research laboratory used by today's scientists. Following in his footsteps, inventors are busy working on things to make our lives better. But, even today, Thomas Alva Edison is still the champ!

Comprehension-Boosting Crosswords: Famous Americans © 2008 by Sylvia Charlesworth, Scholastic Teaching Resources

Name _____

Thomas Alva Edison

DOWN

1. _____ is another name for "sweat."

2. When trains wait in the station before their next run, it's called a _____.

3. Thomas Edison gave his _____ a lot of credit for his success.

6. A "candy _____" sold newspapers and refreshments on trains.

7. Thomas Edison had 1,093 _____ on his different inventions.

8. Alexander Graham Bell and Edison both worked on the _____.

11. Edison was so busy inventing, he went for _____ with little food or sleep.

14. Edison thought of the idea of having a large _____ laboratory.

18. A _____ is a magician or sorcerer.

ACROSS

4. Tom raised and sold _____ to buy chemicals for his basement lab.

5. Edison believed in hard _____.

9. Edison invented the _____, which came long before CD players.

10. The "Wizard of _____ Park" was a nickname Edison didn't like.

12. Before the invention of the radio or telephone, a _____ would send messages over wires by tapping out letters using dots and dashes (Morse code).

13. The *Grand Trunk Herald* was the name of Tom's own _____.

15. Tom saved the stationmaster's _____ from a runaway boxcar (freight car).

16. More than _____ hundred of Edison's patents were related to electricity.

17. Thomas Alva Edison was born in 1847 in Milan, _____.

19. An _____ lamp is the old-fashioned name for an electric light bulb.

20. West _____, New Jersey, was the site of Edison's last research laboratory.

Comprehension-Boosting Crosswords: Famous Americans © 2008 by Sylvia Charlesworth, Scholastic Teaching Resources

Benjamin Franklin
Printer, Writer, Inventor, Statesman

Benjamin Franklin was one of 17 children. With so many mouths to feed, money was scarce, and his father, Josiah, a candlemaker, hoped Ben would become a minister. But Ben had a different idea. At a young age he became an apprentice (helper who wants to learn a trade) to his half-brother, who was a printer. After a time, he decided to move to Philadelphia to start his own printing business. Hardworking, dedicated, and very successful, Ben loved Philadelphia—and the city loves him to this very day. In fact, each January, the Franklin Institute, a science museum, throws a "Birthday Bash" to celebrate Franklin's life.

Born: January 17, 1706, in Boston, Massachusetts

Died: April 17, 1790, in Philadelphia, Pennsylvania

Famous for: being a Founding Father, a man of wisdom and many talents

Ben Franklin accomplished so many important things in his lifetime that it's difficult to list them all. Of course, he helped write the Declaration of Independence and our Constitution. He also founded the University of Pennsylvania and served as deputy postmaster to the colonies. His printing shop in Philadelphia published *The Pennsylvania Gazette* and *Poor Richard's Almanack*, a book that contained some of Ben's wise sayings. One of his favorites was "A penny saved is a penny earned." In honor of this famous adage, a bust of Franklin was made from 80,000 copper pennies collected by schoolchildren.

Franklin was also an experimenter and an inventor. Famous for flying a kite in a thunderstorm, he proved lightning and electricity are the same thing. He invented the stove that bears his name, which gives off more heat than a fireplace. Responsible for creating bifocal eyeglasses, he invented them because he wanted to see both near and far. Credit Ben with the rocking chair and the odometer (an instrument that measures distance traveled by a vehicle). A library, a hospital, a fire department, and the American Philosophical Society were all begun by Benjamin Franklin.

Franklin spent years in France, and he persuaded the French to support the colonists' fight for independence. France helped in a big way with money and the use of its navy. When Franklin died at the age of 84 in Philadelphia, 20,000 people went to his funeral. Many people in France wore black armbands in mourning. By just about any measure, Ben's life was a successful one. Still, he had regrets. He broke relations with his son William, who supported England and was against America's independence. He also failed to get slavery outlawed, although it was a cause he'd worked hard for. Nevertheless, Benjamin Franklin lived a full life, and no doubt followed some of his own best advice: "Early to bed and early to rise, makes a man healthy, wealthy and wise."

DOWN

1. Benjamin Franklin was born in _____, Massachusetts, in 1706.

2. An _____ is a wise saying, maxim, or proverb.

3. Schoolchildren donated 80,000 _____ pennies for a bust of Ben.

5. Ben Franklin proved lightning and _____ were the same thing.

6. Ben Franklin was apprenticed to his half-brother's _____ shop.

7. For a while, Josiah (Ben's father) wanted him to be a _____.

8. Ben was one of _____ children.

10. _____ supported the cause of our independence with money and its navy.

13. The Franklin _____ provided more heat than a fireplace.

14. Ben published *The Pennsylvania Gazette* and *Poor Richard's* _____.

16. When Ben was young, _____ was scarce in his big family.

ACROSS

1. The Franklin Institute has a "_____ Bash" each January.

4. One of Ben's many activities was to be deputy _____.

9. Ben was one of the authors of the Declaration of _____.

11. The _____ of Pennsylvania was founded by Ben Franklin.

12. "A penny saved is a _____ earned," Ben said.

15. Ben Franklin worked hard, to no avail, to abolish _____.

17. An _____ measures distance traveled by a vehicle.

18. Benjamin Franklin wanted our country to be independent of _____.

19. Ben needed _____ (glasses that see near and far), so he invented them.

Thomas Jefferson
Architect of Democracy

Thomas Jefferson was the main author of the Declaration of Independence, and he died on the 50th anniversary of its signing. In an even stranger coincidence, another Founding Father and contributor to the Declaration, John Adams, died on the exact same day, July 4, 1826. Jefferson was an old man, and he'd already designed his own tombstone. It was to be in the shape of an obelisk, and it should have "the following inscription and not a word more: Here was buried Thomas Jefferson, Author of the Declaration of American Independence, of the Statute of Virginia for religious freedom, and father of the University of Virginia." A tombstone big enough to list all Jefferson's accomplishments would have been gigantic. He was brilliant, and more than anyone else, he forged our country's democracy.

Born: April 13, 1743, in Albemarle County, Virginia

Died: July 4, 1826, at Monticello, his Virginia estate

Famous for: writing our Declaration of Independence; being our third President

Jefferson had confidence that educated people could govern themselves wisely. In fact, he believed that education was the foundation of democracy. Believing in the "common" man, he advocated making education available to the general public and founded the University of Virginia. He enjoyed the exchange of ideas and didn't get upset when people disagreed with him. A big reader and deep thinker, he owned a vast quantity of books. After the British burned our Library of Congress (War of 1812), he sold his huge collection of books to the United States.

A big proponent of liberty, religious freedom was very important to Jefferson. He wanted to make sure that people were free to practice their own faith. Though he was not an especially good public speaker, his words were beautifully crafted. Even today, these words from the Declaration of Independence inspire people all over the world: "We hold these truths to be self-evident, that all men are created equal, that they are endowed by their Creator with certain unalienable Rights, that among these are Life, Liberty and the pursuit of Happiness."

One of the major achievements of his presidency was the Louisiana Purchase. Afraid that the United States was vulnerable to foreign rulers, Jefferson paid Napoleon $15 million for the land, which doubled the size of the country. Then he sent the Lewis and Clark Expedition to map and document what he had bought.

Jefferson retired to his country estate at Monticello, which he designed himself. Architecture was another of his varied interests. His accomplishments were many, but he regretted that he didn't succeed in ending slavery. Despite some other disappointments, he said, "My confidence in my countrymen generally leaves me without much fear for the future." Today, we can take comfort from those words.

Comprehension-Boosting Crosswords: Famous Americans © 2008 by Sylvia Charlesworth, Scholastic Teaching Resources

DOWN

1. A tapering four-sided shaft of stone with a pyramid on top is an _____.

3. Thomas Jefferson designed and built his estate called _____.

4. Although he was an inspiring _____, Jefferson was not a great speaker.

5. Jefferson was opposed to _____, which he thought was bad for everyone.

7. The U.S. fought the _____ a second time during the War of 1812.

8. Jefferson bought the Louisiana Purchase from the French leader_____.

9. John _____ and Jefferson both died on the 50th anniversary of the Declaration of Independence (1826).

12. _____ is an old-fashioned word meaning "absolute, incapable of being taken away."

14. Jefferson had _____ that educated people would govern themselves wisely.

15. William _____ and Meriwether Lewis led the exploration of the West.

16. Jefferson sold the U.S. government his huge _____ of books.

ACROSS

2. _____ freedom was extremely important to Thomas Jefferson.

6. The _____ Purchase doubled the size of our country (at that time).

10. Old buildings and the study of _____ fascinated Thomas Jefferson.

11. _____ is the foundation of democracy, Jefferson believed.

13. More than anyone, Jefferson forged our _____.

17. Jefferson founded the University of _____.

18. The main author of our _____ of Independence was Thomas Jefferson.

19. The Louisiana Purchase cost fifteen _____ dollars.

20. The British burned our Library of _____ to the ground.

Helen Keller
Inspiration for the World

A scene in *The Miracle Worker* (which was both a play and a movie about the life of Helen Keller) shows the moment when Helen's mother, Kate, realizes her child can't hear. Kate utters a scream that pierces the audience's heart. Helen Adams Keller was born beautiful, healthy, and very high-spirited. At the age of 19 months, she got very sick, and was left deaf, dumb (unable to speak clearly), and blind. Her parents, who were caring but very upset, let Helen do whatever she wanted. She snatched food off other people's plates, threw tantrums, and locked her mother in the pantry. Because she was an infant when she became ill, she had no memory of speech or of what things looked like. She careened (lurched) about in a totally dark and silent world, unable to communicate easily with others. She did develop her own language of sorts, containing about 60 gestures. If she wanted buttered bread she pantomimed (acted out with no sound) slicing and buttering the bread.

Born: June 27, 1880, in Tuscumbia, Alabama

Died: June 1, 1968, in Westport, Connecticut

Famous for: helping and inspiring all people, despite being blind and deaf

By chance, her mother read the book *American Notes* by Charles Dickens. Dickens wrote about Laura Bridgman, also blind and deaf, who had been taught a "manual alphabet." It allowed her to "talk" by tracing letters on the palm of the hand of someone who knew the alphabet (and vice versa). Also, Helen met inventor Alexander Graham Bell, who had a lifelong interest in helping the deaf. He helped persuade Annie Sullivan, who was the "miracle worker," to go to Tuscumbia, where the Kellers lived, to teach Helen. Annie, half blind herself, had grown up in the Tewksbury, Massachusetts, poorhouse. But she had convinced the authorities to send her to the school for the blind. It was there she learned the skills that would later help Helen.

In the beginning, the job with Helen was very rough on everyone. Teacher and pupil withdrew to a separate "Little House." Annie imposed discipline and taught Helen tirelessly. Finally, one day, a breakthrough came. While holding Helen's hand under the spout, Annie pumped some water, and at the same time spelled *w-a-t-e-r* in Helen's hand. At last, Helen understood. She was able to make the connection between the water and the word "spelled" in her hand. After that, there was no stopping her! In 1904, she graduated from Radcliffe College. A successful author, she also appeared on stage and in a movie. She raised money for the American Foundation for the Blind. She loved to meet people and travel and was always open to new ideas. As she put it, "I am constantly on the lookout for miracles. The unexpected might happen at any odd moment, and I want to be on the spot."

Comprehension-Boosting Crosswords: Famous Americans © 2008 by Sylvia Charlesworth, Scholastic Teaching Resources

Name _____

Helen Keller

DOWN

1. Helen Keller learned to communicate by using the _____ alphabet.

2. At first, Annie and Helen lived in the "_____ House."

3. Helen's teacher was named Annie _____.

6. Illness left Helen blind, _____, and unable to speak.

7. Annie's parents left her and her brother in the Tewksbury _____.

8. Charles _____ wrote about Laura Bridgman, who learned the manual alphabet.

14. *The Miracle* _____ was a stage play and a movie.

16. Helen once locked her mother in the _____ (storage area near kitchen).

ACROSS

4. Vice _____ means with the order reversed.

5. Helen Keller was a 1904 graduate of _____ College.

7. An outdoor hand water _____ provided the first sign that Helen understood words.

9. Helen Adams Keller was born in _____, Alabama, in 1880.

10. Helen loved to _____ and visited many places and met lots of people.

11. When she died, Helen Keller was not quite 88 years _____.

12. Helen was ". . . constantly on the lookout for _____."

13. Alexander Graham _____, a friend of Helen's, invented the telephone.

15. When someone uses gestures but no words to act out an idea, it's called _____.

17. A successful _____, Helen also gave lectures, and was in a movie.

18. When Helen was _____ months old, she became seriously ill.

19. Helen died in Westport, _____, in 1968.

Dr. Martin Luther King, Jr.
Champion of Civil Rights

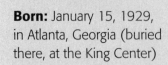

The date was August 28, 1963. It was hot, and a crowd of over 250,000 people had gathered around the Lincoln Memorial in Washington, D.C. They had come to march for racial equality, and by three o'clock they were tired. But they waited to hear the last speaker, Dr. Martin Luther King, Jr., address the crowd. Dr. King began to read from his prepared text. Then, his heart took over and he put down his notes. He gave a speech, which is one of the most famous ever delivered. "So I say to you today, my friends, that even though we face the difficulties of today and tomorrow, I still have a dream. It is a dream rooted in the American dream.. . ." He continued, ". . . from every mountainside, let freedom ring." His dream was that African Americans and all people would be treated equally under the law, and thus enjoy equal opportunities.

Born: January 15, 1929, in Atlanta, Georgia (buried there, at the King Center)

Died: April 4, 1968, on the balcony of the Lorraine Motel, Memphis, Tennessee

Famous for: leading the civil rights movement

What was so extraordinary about this man? A powerful orator with a beautiful voice, he used his gift of speech with great skill. His cadence (musical beat) and way with words built his speeches to a stirring climax and pulled his listeners in. An experienced preacher, he believed in his message so deeply that his audience was often moved to tears. But he was more than a great speaker. He was educated, principled, and courageous. He knew how to organize effectively, was a hard worker, and understood how to time his protests and get lots of people involved. In Birmingham, Alabama, he encouraged children to march for freedom. When police dogs and fire hoses were turned on them, the assaults were shown on TV, and the world saw the brutality of segregation.

King was a devoted follower of a nonviolent approach, and he encouraged people to examine their consciences and then do the right thing. More than once he went to jail for his activism. Supporting the concept of civil disobedience, he believed that obeying unjust laws was wrong. Gradually, many people saw that he was right. More than any other person, Dr. King is responsible for the gains African Americans have made in winning their civil rights. He was awarded the 1964 Nobel Peace Prize, a very high honor.

On April 3, 1968, Dr. King addressed a crowd in Memphis, Tennessee. Very tired, he gave a speech saying he had been "allowed . . . to go up to the mountain" and there he had "seen the Promised Land." By this he meant a day when the fight for equality had been won and all people lived in peace and harmony. Tragically, Dr. King was shot and killed the next day, leaving his wife Coretta Scott King, four children, and a grieving nation. A national holiday celebrates his inspiring life and many accomplishments.

Name _____

DOWN

1. Dr. King's "I Have a _____" speech is famous the world over.

3. Children were sprayed with fire hoses during a protest march in _____, Alabama.

5. After he was arrested, Dr. King was sent to _____.

8. Dr. Martin Luther King, Jr. is buried at the King _____ in Atlanta, Georgia.

9. Anyone who heard him speak knew that King was a powerful _____.

11. The night before he died, Dr. King said he had seen the _____ Land.

12. King and his supporters believed in the principles of non-_____ protest.

13. The _____ Dream is the idea that everyone, regardless of race, can have a good life if they work hard.

ACROSS

2. The _____ Peace Prize was awarded to Dr. King in Oslo, Norway, in 1964.

4. The _____ Motel, where Dr. King died, is now a museum.

6. _____ Scott King married Dr. King in 1953, and they had four children.

7. _____ is the balanced rhythmic flow of music, poetry, or oratory.

10. King's "I Have a Dream" speech was given at the _____ Memorial.

14. Martin Luther King, Jr. was only _____-nine when he was killed.

15. Others besides Dr. King were opposed to the _____ of black Americans.

16. Dr. King wanted people to examine their _____ and do the right thing.

17. _____ disobedience means not obeying laws one feels are unjust.

18. ". . . from every mountainside, let _____ ring," said Dr. King.

19. Dr. King was born in _____, Georgia.

20. We celebrate Dr. King's life each year with a national _____.

Meriwether Lewis & William Clark
Intrepid Explorers

Born: Lewis, August 18, 1774;
Clark, August 1, 1770 (both in
Virginia)

Died: Lewis, September 1809,
in Tennessee; Clark, September
1838, in Missouri

Famous for: leading the Corps
of Discovery (Lewis and Clark
Expedition)

These are the words Captain William Clark wrote in his
journal on November 7, 1805, after seeing the Pacific
Ocean for the first time: "Ocian in view! O! the joy." (His
spelling of "ocean" was not how we spell it today.) Clark,
along with Captain Meriwether Lewis and the rest of
their party, had just completed a remarkable undertaking.
They had traveled mostly overland from Missouri to what
is now the state of Oregon. For much of the trip, they
were accompanied by a Shoshone Indian Sacagawea;
her husband, Toussaint Charbonneau; and their baby,
Jean Baptiste (nicknamed Pomp). In all, Lewis and Clark
traveled for nearly three years. They began in St. Louis in the winter of 1803, headed west to the
Pacific, and returned to St. Louis, to cheering crowds, on September 23, 1806.

Exploration of the West had been a longtime dream of President Jefferson. He and others
sought a water route (by boat only) to the Pacific coast. Jefferson feared the French or Spanish
might sail up the Mississippi River from New Orleans and take over our western territories. After
the English explorer Alexander Mackenzie went through British America (now Canada) to the
Pacific, Jefferson worried about the British, too. He offered to buy land from France's Napoleon,
and was amazed to be offered a huge piece of land, today known as the Louisiana Purchase, for
only fifteen million dollars. He accepted, and instantly doubled the size of our country. The land
extended from the Mississippi River to the Rocky Mountains, and from the Gulf of Mexico to
Canada. It was a vast wilderness, and Jefferson wanted to find out everything he could about it.

He put Meriwether Lewis in charge of the expedition, known as the Corps of Discovery.
Lewis chose his good friend William Clark as his co-captain. The rest of the team, 33 recruits,
were well-disciplined soldiers. Despite extreme hardship, only one man was lost (he died from
appendicitis). Lewis did much of the advance planning and took courses in ecology so he could
identify the flora (plants) and fauna (animals) they encountered. Clark, the practical engineer,
was more disciplined about keeping a journal. The two designed special boats and went up the
Missouri River. After building Fort Mandan (in North Dakota) near an Indian village, they spent
the winter there. Next came the difficult passage through the Rockies, walking and using horses,
on their journey to the Pacific. Before turning back, they spent another winter on the coast (at
Fort Clatsop). In their travels, they came to know Native Americans, "respect" grizzly bears,
love prairie dogs, and hate mosquitoes. The year 2003 marked the 200th anniversary of their
magnificent journey.

Meriwether Lewis and William Clark

DOWN

1. President Thomas _____ wanted the West explored.

3. Sergeant Charles Floyd, the only man lost, died from _____.

4. Jefferson acquired the _____ Purchase from Napoleon.

6. 2003 marked the 200th _____ of the Lewis and Clark Expedition.

9. Sacagawea's baby, Jean Baptiste, was nicknamed _____.

11. A Shoshone Indian woman named _____ joined the Corps of Discovery.

13. In his journal Clark spelled _____ "Ocian".

16. The members of the Corps of Discovery were in the U.S. _____.

19. The Lewis and Clark Expedition returned to cheering throngs in St. _____.

ACROSS

2. Captain Lewis chose William _____ to co-command the Expedition.

5. Alexander _____ reached the Pacific Ocean from Canada in 1793.

7. Lewis and Clark met the Pacific Ocean in what today is the state of _____.

8. The Lewis and Clark _____ began in the winter of 1803-04.

10. The Expedition lasted more than three _____ (including plans and preparations).

12. The Expedition's leaders were William Clark and _____ Lewis.

14. The official name of the group was the Corps _____ Discovery.

15. Lewis and Clark were both called "_____" by their men.

17. The word _____ means animal life.

18. The Corps of Discovery learned to fear and respect _____ bears.

20. The word _____ refers to plant life.

Abraham Lincoln
The Great Emancipator

On November 19, 1863, Abraham Lincoln spoke at the dedication of the national cemetery at Gettysburg (Pennsylvania). The Battle of Gettysburg had turned the tide of the Civil War in favor of the North. With 50,000 casualties at that battle alone (dead and wounded), Lincoln's heart was heavy. He gave one of the most famous speeches of all time. His "Gettysburg Address" began: "Fourscore and seven years ago our fathers brought forth on this continent a new nation, conceived in liberty, and dedicated to the proposition that all men are created equal." After speaking for about two minutes, he ended, saying: ". . . that we here highly resolve that these dead shall not have died in vain; . . . and that government of the people, by the people, and for the people shall not perish from the earth."

Born: February 12, 1809, in Hardin County, Kentucky

Died: April 15, 1865, in Washington, D.C. (buried in Springfield, Illinois)

Famous for: being the 16th President, freeing the slaves, and ending the Civil War

The Lincoln Memorial in Washington, D.C., portrays a serious and contemplative (thinking) Lincoln. Born poor to frontier farmers, Abraham Lincoln was fiercely ambitious. Growing up, he was determined to educate himself, and as he worked in the fields, he propped a book up on his plow. At night he read by the glow of the fireplace. Very tall and very thin, Lincoln was known for his incredible strength and skill with an ax. Even though he was well liked, and had a quick sense of humor, he was highly critical of himself. He worked splitting timber, as a boatman on the Mississippi River, as a storekeeper, and as a postmaster. He wanted to be a lawyer, and passed the Illinois bar exam without ever going to law school.

In 1858, Lincoln decided to run against Stephen A. Douglas for the U.S. Senate. The candidates agreed to a series of seven debates, mainly over the issue of slavery. Lincoln argued against extending slavery to any U.S. territory not yet a state. Brilliant and inspiring, Abraham Lincoln was soon famous (although he lost the election). Committed to preserving the Union at all costs, Lincoln was chosen as the first Republican candidate to run for President. In 1860 he won that election. Lincoln despaired when the South fired on Fort Sumter in April of 1861, which marked the start of our Civil War. As the war progressed, Lincoln became more determined to abolish slavery. He issued the Emancipation Proclamation (1863), which freed the slaves. The Thirteenth Amendment to our Constitution (1865) made it official.

In his second inaugural address, Lincoln promised to bind up the nation's wounds "with malice toward none; with charity for all." It was not to be. Five days after the South's General Robert E. Lee surrendered, ending the war (1865), Lincoln and his wife, Mary Todd, celebrated at Ford's Theater. A crazed actor, John Wilkes Booth, entered the President's theater box and shot him. Abraham Lincoln died the next day, leaving a grieving and seriously wounded nation.

Comprehension-Boosting Crosswords: Famous Americans © 2008 by Sylvia Charlesworth, Scholastic Teaching Resources

Name _____

Abraham Lincoln

DOWN

1. Lincoln passed the Illinois bar and became a successful _____.

2. To _____ means to set free, to liberate.

3. Lincoln had four children with his wife, _____ Todd Lincoln.

5. Skilled with an _____, Lincoln cleared farmland and split timber.

6. Lincoln's tomb (as well as the only home Lincoln ever owned) is in _____, Illinois.

7. The U.S. _____ War is also called the War Between the States.

8. Stephen A. _____ and Abraham Lincoln had seven famous debates.

11. Lincoln was determined to preserve the _____ at all costs.

14. Lincoln and his wife attended the _____ to celebrate the war's end.

16. John Wilkes _____ assassinated Lincoln in Ford's Theater.

ACROSS

1. Robert E. _____ surrendered to General Grant at Appomattox Court House.

4. Lincoln was named for his grandfather, _____.

9. Lincoln was born in the state of _____.

10. Lincoln had a good sense of _____, although he worried and brooded.

12. Lincoln worked as a boatman on the _____.

13. There were almost 50,000 casualties (both sides) at _____, where Lincoln gave his famous address.

15. _____ means the desire to harm others; charity means love and good will.

17. The Thirteenth _____ to our Constitution outlaws slavery.

18. In Washington, the Lincoln _____ faces the Washington Monument.

19. The Civil War began when the South fired on Fort _____.

Thurgood Marshall
Justice for All

Thurgood Marshall was named "Thoroughgood" after his father's father. When he learned to write, he shortened it to "Thurgood," saying his real name was "too long." Unusual names, such as "Thornygood" and "Olive Branch," were sprinkled throughout his family. So were strong personalities. His great-grandfather was born a slave but given his freedom. His grandparents on both sides had reputations as fighters for their rights. Thurgood's own father taught him to use his fists, if anyone ever called him an insulting name. Taking that advice nearly landed Thurgood in jail. He thought things over and decided to use the law to ensure fair treatment for himself, other African Americans, and all Americans.

Born: July 2, 1908, in Baltimore, Maryland

Died: January 24, 1993, at Bethesda Naval Medical Center in Maryland

Famous for: being the first black jurist to serve on the U.S. Supreme Court

As punishment for bad behavior or not paying attention in class, Thurgood was often sent to the school's basement. He was told to memorize, and then he had to recite, long portions of our Constitution. The principal probably didn't know it, but he had provided the pathway for Thurgood. Starting out as an attorney for the NAACP (National Association for the Advancement of Colored People), he eventually argued 31 cases before our top court, the U.S. Supreme Court. He won 29 of those cases. In 1954, Thurgood Marshall won the landmark case *Brown v. Board of Education of Topeka*. After demonstrating that the law of "separate but equal" was unconstitutional, and outright harmful, the Supreme Court ordered the desegregation of all public schools. Thurgood really knew his Constitution!

Marshall attended all-black Lincoln University near Oxford, Pennsylvania. While there, he and some fellow students demanded equal access at their local movie house. They peaceably forced the management to allow African-American students out of the balcony, where they'd been forced to sit. Thurgood graduated at the head of his class, with a law degree, from another all-black school named Howard University in Washington, D.C. He set up a law practice in Baltimore, but after three years began work for the NAACP. President Kennedy appointed him to the U.S. Court of Appeals in 1961. In 1965, President Lyndon Baines Johnson appointed him Solicitor General (the top U.S. attorney), and then (in 1967) to the Supreme Court. When Justice Marshall was preparing to leave our highest court, an admiring student, interviewing him, expressed regret that he was retiring. But by then, he was in his eighties, and had given many years of service to our country. Throughout his life, Thurgood Marshall worked hard to help African Americans gain equality and truly earned his nickname—"Mr. Civil Rights."

Name _____

DOWN

1. After twenty-four _____ on the Supreme Court, Justice Marshall retired.

2. Thurgood and his friends resented having to sit in the _____ at the movies.

4. Thurgood learned that using his _____ was a risky way to fight for his rights.

6. President _____ Baines Johnson appointed Marshall to the top court.

9. Thurgood's given name, which he said was "too long," was _____.

11. _____ was *not* equal, argued Marshall before the Supreme Court.

13. _____ University was where Thurgood spent his undergraduate years.

16. President John F. _____ appointed Marshall to the Court of Appeals.

18. Thurgood's grandfather had the middle name _____ Branch (for peace).

ACROSS

3. The Solicitor _____ is the top attorney for the U.S. government.

5. Thurgood Marshall's nickname was "Mr. _____ Rights."

7. Marshall won 29 of the 31 _____ he argued before the Supreme Court.

8. As a punishment, the principal made Thurgood learn and recite the _____.

10. _____ of the public schools was accomplished through lawsuits.

12. The first black _____ on the Supreme Court was Thurgood Marshall.

14. Other members of Thurgood's family were _____ for justice.

15. Marshall earned his law degree at _____ University.

17. _____, Maryland, was the city where Thurgood was born.

19. Marshall argued the landmark case *Brown v. Board of _____ of Topeka.*

20. _____ stands for the National Association for the Advancement of Colored People.

John Muir
Guardian of the Wilderness

John Muir had a powerful relationship with the earth. He felt deeply connected to everything in nature—the sunshine, a drop of water, and every blade of grass. The natural world inspired wonder in him, and he once said that when in nature, "One learns that the world though made, is yet being made. That this is still the morning of creation." Especially drawn to mountains and the high country, he was exhilarated by the cold and loved the beauty and purity of glaciers. He showed reverence for all creatures, from a tiny beetle to a gigantic whale. Feeling the awesome force of nature throughout the wilderness, he drew strength from it, saying he had never seen "an ugly landscape." In fact, in the low country away from the mountains or in "civilization," he often got sick. His lungs began to bother him and he would announce, "The mountains are calling me and I must go." Sleeping in snow and eating hardtack and water would restore him.

Born: April 21, 1838, in Dunbar, Scotland

Died: December 24, 1914, in Los Angeles, California

Famous for: protecting Yosemite and Sequoia National Parks; founding the Sierra Club

Muir was thin, bearded, and often disheveled (messy). Yet, he was incredibly strong. Setting off alone on foot, he could trek a distance of a thousand miles. After scaling Mt. Rainier, he said, "I did not mean to climb it, but got excited and soon was at the top." Muir knew that a connection to nature was important for all of us. As he put it, "Everybody needs beauty as well as bread, places to play in and pray in, where Nature may heal and cheer and give strength to body and soul." Because he felt this so strongly, he worked relentlessly to document and preserve our priceless wild places.

John Muir was born in Dunbar, Scotland. The family consisted of his father, Daniel, his mother, Ann, and seven siblings (one was born in America). His father was strict, and the children worked hard. The family moved to a farm in Wisconsin, and John went to the University of Wisconsin when he grew up. A talented inventor, he also was interested in botany and geology. While working in a factory, he had a serious accident, which almost left him blind. When his sight improved, he decided to go exploring while he could still see and savor the world around him. His travels eventually brought him to Yosemite, a place of breathtaking beauty in California that he would be devoted to for the rest of his life. John married Louie Strentzel, who understood his need to explore. But as he got older, he spent more time writing about his experiences, and enjoying their two daughters. He left us a legacy of appreciation, and the idea that we should actively seek to protect our beautiful land. Muir Woods near San Francisco and the Muir Glacier in Alaska honor his name.

Comprehension-Boosting Crosswords: Famous Americans © 2008 by Sylvia Charlesworth, Scholastic Teaching Resources

Name _____

DOWN

1. John Muir's father was very _____ with his eight children.

2. John Muir said, "Everybody needs _____ as well as bread. . . ."

4. "The _____ are calling me and I must go," John would announce.

7. Muir was born in Dunbar, _____.

9. Although John was a talented _____, he preferred to be outdoors.

10. There is a glacier in _____ named for Muir, who explored that state.

13. The _____ Club, founded by John Muir and others, seeks to protect the environment.

15. Although Mt. _____ is a challenging climb, Muir scaled it easily.

ACROSS

3. Muir was a gifted _____ who left us many books to enjoy.

5. Near San _____ there is a forest of coastal redwoods called Muir Woods.

6. After a factory accident, John thought he would be _____ forever.

8. John Muir thought that every day was ". . . still the morning of _____."

11. _____ National Park probably owes its existence to John Muir.

12. Muir was so strong and able that he could easily manage a thousand-mile _____.

13. _____ National Park was another place Muir worked to preserve.

14. John Muir was thin, had a _____, and was sometimes in tattered clothes.

16. The Muir family moved to _____ and had a farm there.

17. Muir had a passion for _____ because they were pure and beautiful.

18. John Muir died of pneumonia in a hospital in Los _____, California.

19. John Muir and his wife, Louie Strentzel, had two _____.

Rosa Parks
Civil Rights Activist

It is often said that Rosa Parks (born Rosa McCauley) was too tired after a hard day's work to stand up and give her bus seat to a white man. In her book *My Story* (written with Jim Haskins), she sets the record straight. On that momentous day (December 1, 1955) Rosa was indeed tired, "tired of giving in." Many black Americans rode the buses in Montgomery, the capital of Alabama. Forced to pay in the front, they then had to get off the bus and enter the rear door to sit or stand in the "black section." A particularly mean bus driver could take off before they had time to get back on, leaving them stranded. It was not planned, but Rosa thought her actions through very carefully. When the bus driver told her she would be arrested if she didn't give up her seat, she said, "You may do that." Then she waited for the police to come and take her to jail. She was tried and found guilty. Asked to be the plaintiff (person bringing a lawsuit) in a court case challenging segregation, she agreed. Dignified, intelligent, and brave, she was the perfect person for a test case.

Born: February 4, 1913, in Tuskegee, Alabama

Died: October 24, 2005 (at the age of 92), in Detroit, Michigan

Famous for: refusing a bus driver's order to give up her seat to a white man

Meanwhile, following Rosa's arrest, Dr. Martin Luther King Jr. organized the Montgomery bus boycott, which lasted 381 days. With considerable hardship, blacks walked to work. At the boycott's end, the U.S. Supreme Court had declared segregation on city buses illegal. With Dr. King at the forefront, the mass movement of nonviolent protests to end such injustices had begun. They continued throughout the 1960s. Rosa Parks brought passion to the fight. She was married to Raymond Parks, an active member of the NAACP (National Association for the Advancement of Colored People), the oldest civil rights organization in the U.S. (founded in 1909). As secretary of that group, Rosa twice tried, unsuccessfully, to register to vote. Finally, on the third try, she succeeded. In 1963, she attended the giant civil rights march on Washington, and spoke at the Southern Christian Leadership Council's annual convention. Ten years after the famous bus incident, Rosa took a job in Detroit working for Congressman John Conyers, one of the few African-American politicians at the time.

The historic bus Rosa rode (redone to look exactly as it did that memorable December day) is on display at the Henry Ford Museum in Dearborn, Michigan. There is a bust of her at the Smithsonian Institution. She was awarded the Presidential Medal of Freedom (1996) and Congressional Gold Medal (1999). But she was most proud of the Rosa and Raymond Parks Institute of Self-Development, founded to promote career training for black youth. At her death she was the first woman to lie in state (for two days) in the rotunda of the U.S. Capitol. Rosa Parks achieved a great deal for a "tired" seamstress from Alabama.

DOWN

1. For 23 years, Rosa Parks worked for Congressman _____ Conyers.

2. On _____ 1, 1955, Rosa Parks refused to give up her bus seat.

5. The U.S. Supreme Court declared _____ on city buses illegal.

7. The person who brings a lawsuit to court is called a _____.

10. Rosa Parks was tried and found _____.

12. Rosa Parks was born Rosa McCauley in _____, Alabama.

13. Dr. _____ Luther King Jr. helped organize the Montgomery bus boycott.

16. With Jim Haskins, Rosa Parks wrote her autobiography, called *My* _____.

17. _____ stands for National Association for the Advancement of Colored People.

ACROSS

3. To _____ means to refuse to use or buy something as a means of protest.

4. In 1999, Rosa Parks received a high honor, the _____ Gold Medal.

6. The capital of the state of Alabama is _____.

8. Rosa's famous bus is in the Henry Ford Museum in _____, Michigan.

9. The bus _____ had Rosa arrested when she remained in her seat.

11. In 1963, there was a huge civil rights march on _____.

14. On the _____ try, Rosa voted successfully, having been refused twice.

15. Rosa Parks said she was "_____ of giving in."

16. There is a bust of Rosa Parks at the _____ Institution.

18. Rosa was working as a _____ in Montgomery, Alabama.

19. The Montgomery bus boycott was the first of many nonviolent _____.

Eleanor Roosevelt
Stateswoman of the World

"Where she walked, beauty was always there. She did not despair of the darkness. She lit a candle. Her glow has warmed the world." Our ambassador to the United Nations, Adlai Stevenson, spoke these words after Eleanor Roosevelt's death. As a child, Anna Eleanor Roosevelt did not feel beautiful. Painfully shy, she was ashamed of her appearance—she thought her teeth stuck out. Her own mother nicknamed her "Granny." Born rich and privileged in New York City, she adored her father, Elliott, but he was in poor health and died when Eleanor was 9. When her mother also got sick and died, Eleanor, at age 10, was an orphan left in the care of her "no-nonsense" grandmother.

Born: October 11, 1884, in New York

Died: November 7, 1962, in New York

Famous for: being an active First Lady, writer, lecturer, diplomat, and humanitarian

Sent to boarding school in England, she was smart, disciplined, and an excellent student. On returning home, like other wealthy young women of that time, she was expected to attend fancy parties and do charity work. There was to be no college for Eleanor. But helping the less fortunate made a lasting impression on her. Compassionate and caring, she soon started impressing her handsome, popular, distant cousin, Franklin Delano Roosevelt (often called FDR). He enjoyed sharing ideas with her. The two courted and eventually married on St. Patrick's Day, 1905. Her uncle, President Theodore Roosevelt, gave her away.

Eleanor and Franklin had five children. The family spent summers on Campobello Island in Canada. One day in 1921, after a swim, Franklin became sick with polio. He spent the rest of his life in a wheelchair. His powerful mother, Sara, wanted him to retire, but Eleanor insisted that her husband resume his political life. In 1932, FDR was elected President. He held the office for four terms, spanning the Great Depression and most of World War II. Acting as his eyes, ears, and legs, Eleanor traveled where FDR couldn't. At times, she became his conscience, urging him to do the right thing. Overcoming her own fears, she gave speeches, spoke on the radio, and wrote books and a newspaper column. During the war, she flew to distant battlefields, paying visits to the servicemen. After her husband died in office, the new President, Harry Truman, appointed her a delegate to the United Nations. There she wrote (with others) the Universal Declaration of Human Rights. In 1961, President Kennedy asked her to serve the UN again (the National Commission on the Status of Women). Eleanor Roosevelt's greatest achievement was being a humanitarian, working for the betterment of all people everywhere.

Comprehension-Boosting Crosswords: Famous Americans © 2008 by Sylvia Charlesworth, Scholastic Teaching Resources

Name _____

DOWN

1. President John F. _____ reappointed Eleanor to the United Nations.

2. President Harry _____ made Eleanor Roosevelt a delegate to the UN.

4. Franklin Delano Roosevelt got _____ and afterward was confined to a wheelchair.

5. Eleanor Roosevelt visited many battlefields during _____ War II.

6. President _____ Roosevelt was Eleanor Roosevelt's uncle.

10. From the Great _____ through World War II, Eleanor was First Lady.

12. Eleanor Roosevelt was her husband's eyes, ears, legs, and _____.

14. With others, Eleanor wrote the _____ Declaration of Human Rights.

16. A good student, Eleanor went to boarding school in _____.

ACROSS

3. Anna Eleanor Roosevelt was born in New York and called _____.

7. By the age of 10 both of her parents had died and Eleanor was an _____.

8. Ambassador Stevenson called Eleanor _____, but she never thought she was.

9. Franklin Delano Roosevelt, Eleanor's husband, was often called _____.

11. Eleanor was _____, which means sympathetic and caring.

13. A _____, which describes Eleanor, cares about all people everywhere.

15. Eleanor attended parties and did _____ work, but did not go to college.

17. Eleanor and Franklin raised _____ children.

18. UN is short for _____ Nations.

19. "_____" was a nickname for Eleanor, given by her mother.

20. _____ was Eleanor's powerful mother-in-law.

Theodore Roosevelt
President and Conservationist

Theodore Roosevelt, our 26th President, was like a tornado. Strong and bursting with energy, he always shook things up. But he wasn't always that way. Born with severe asthma, he was frail, nervous, and too sickly to attend school. Teddy, as his friends called him, fought back. Determined to become strong, he drove himself relentlessly. He had a great love of nature and the outdoors. He kept reptiles in his mother's refrigerator and birds in his room. Eventually, he became our country's "conservationist President." A conservationist believes in preserving precious natural resources such as water, wilderness, and wildlife.

Born: October 27, 1858, in New York City

Died: January 6, 1919, at home in Oyster Bay, New York

Famous for: being the 26th President; overseeing the creation of the Panama Canal

Roosevelt's feeling for nature was deeply personal. Tragedy struck when his wife, Alice, and mother, Martha, died on the same day. So he headed west to the Badlands of Dakota. This landscape of windswept rock formations and little vegetation comforted him. Throwing himself into ranching as a way to work out his grief, he learned how to be a regular cowboy. Teddy's energy exhausted ordinary people, but he always put thought and purpose behind his activity.

Educated at Harvard and Columbia Law School, Roosevelt was the author of numerous books on wildlife, hunting, history, and politics. Teddy organized the Rough Riders, a cavalry (horse) unit, and fought in the Spanish-American War. He returned home a hero and was elected the governor of New York, and then vice president of the United States. When President William McKinley was assassinated, he became President, winning election on his own in 1904. His accomplishments included undertaking the building of the Panama Canal, connecting the Atlantic and Pacific oceans. He introduced the idea of government inspections to keep our food safe and declared the United States to be protector of the Western Hemisphere (North, Central, and South America). He passed laws to keep business responsible to citizens. For ending the Russo-Japanese War, Roosevelt earned the Nobel Peace Prize. His efforts in conservation earned him the honor of being the only person to have a National Park named for him—Theodore Roosevelt National Park in the Badlands of North Dakota. A carved likeness of his face, in the company of Lincoln, Washington, and Jefferson, graces Mt. Rushmore in the Black Hills near Keystone, South Dakota.

President Roosevelt had six children—five with his second wife, Edith Kermit Carow. He never lost his love for the joys of childhood. Therefore, it is fitting that the most popular and beloved toy of all time is named for him—the teddy bear.

Comprehension-Boosting Crosswords: Famous Americans © 2008 by Sylvia Charlesworth, Scholastic Teaching Resources

Name _____

Comprehension-Boosting Crosswords
Theodore Roosevelt

DOWN

1. President Roosevelt is responsible for building the _____ Canal.

3. _____ was the name of Roosevelt's first wife.

5. Teddy kept _____ in the family refrigerator when he was a boy.

7. Theodore Roosevelt was noted for being a great _____.

10. The _____ were troops trained to fight on horseback.

12. As a boy, Theodore suffered from severe _____.

14. For ending the Russo-Japanese War, Roosevelt received the _____ Peace Prize.

16. Roosevelt's family home was in _____ Bay, New York.

17. President Roosevelt made laws to keep our _____ safe.

ACROSS

2. One university Roosevelt attended was _____.

4. Roosevelt studied _____ at Columbia University.

6. When President _____ died, Roosevelt became President.

8. The _____ are windswept formations with little vegetation.

9. Teddy Roosevelt, sometimes called T. R., lived to be _____ years old.

11. Teddy went to the _____ Badlands after his wife and mother died.

13. Roosevelt wanted the U.S. to be the protector of the _____ Hemisphere.

15. With his tremendous energy and power, Roosevelt reminded some people of a _____.

18. With his second wife, Edith, Roosevelt had _____ children.

19. The _____ bear is the most popular toy ever made.

20. The Rough _____ was the name of Roosevelt's cavalry unit.

45

Sacagawea (Sah-kah'gah-way'a)
Resourceful Explorer

Sacagawea was born a Shoshone Indian in the late 1780s in what is now Idaho. Shoshones were nomadic Native Americans and moved their tepees frequently to obtain food, following the salmon runs and buffalo migrations. They also knew how to locate edible roots and berries. A peaceable people, they owned and rode horses, which caused other tribes to envy and sometimes prey on them. It was a hard life, which demanded numerous skills to survive. Bird Woman (as Sacagawea's name is sometimes translated) learned these skills well. Still, at age 12, camped near what is now called the Three Forks of the Missouri River, Sacagawea was captured by Hidatsa warriors and taken to their village. There, at the age of 16, she married Toussaint Charbonneau, a French fur trader. In 1805, she gave birth to their son, Jean Baptiste.

Born: around 1789, probably in what is now the state of Idaho

Died: probably around 1812, at Fort Manuel in present-day South Dakota

Famous for: accompanying the Corps of Discovery (Lewis and Clark Expedition)

The Corps of Discovery (Lewis and Clark Expedition) met Sacagawea at Fort Mandan. They built their fort near the villages of the Mandan Indian tribe (in what is now North Dakota). Spending the winter of 1804–05 there, they prepared for the journey ahead. They decided to hire Charbonneau as an interpreter. Clark agreed to it, but worried about having an eight-week-old infant (in a cradleboard) with them on such a hard journey. But he adored the baby he called "Pomp," and had enormous respect for "Janey" (his name for Sacagawea).

Because members of the expedition kept journals, we know just how much Sacagawea contributed to the success of their journey. Her presence smoothed the way for the Corps. Native Americans, seeing a Shoshone woman with her baby, realized the explorers were coming in peace. She was able to communicate with other tribes. Her many examples of loyalty and bravery inspired the men. Knowledge of the wilderness allowed her to obtain food. Keeping her head, she saved papers and supplies when a boat capsized. Though very young when she was taken from her homeland, she remembered the area and guided the expedition through it. Reunited there with her brother Cameahwait, a Shoshone chief, she persuaded him to supply them with horses. William Clark said Sacagawea "deserved a greater reward for her attention and services on that route than we had in our power to give her."

Today, Sacagawea would be stunned by the honors bestowed on her. Statues, place names, and a silver dollar all salute her. Her very name has come to stand for "courage." At a young age she longed to see the Pacific Ocean. Because of her great skill, resourcefulness, and extreme bravery, she got her wish!

Name _____

Comprehension-Boosting Crosswords
Sacagawea

DOWN

2. The name Sacagawea is sometimes translated as _____ Woman.

3. The _____ Indians followed game and possessed horses.

4. Lewis, Clark, and other members of the expedition recorded events in their _____.

6. _____, chief of the Shoshones, was Sacagawea's brother.

7. Sacagawea persuaded her brother to supply the expedition with _____.

9. At the time of the Lewis and Clark Expedition, the West was wilderness and Indian villages, and _____ such as Idaho and South Dakota didn't exist yet.

11. The Shoshones fished for salmon and hunted _____.

12. The word _____ means to overturn, such as a boat.

14. Sacagawea knew how to gather _____ plants, roots, and berries.

16. Lewis and Clark built Fort _____ near the Mandan Indian villages.

ACROSS

1. Sacagawea carried her baby in a _____ on her back.

5. Shoshones were _____, which means they moved from place to place.

8. William Clark nicknamed Jean Baptiste, Sacagawea's baby, "_____."

10. A fur trader, Sacagawea's husband was Toussaint _____.

13. When there are no written records, birth and death _____ are sometimes approximations (good guesses).

15. Migratory Indians used portable tents called _____.

17. When she was about 12 years old, _____ warriors captured Sacagawea.

18. Sacagawea's likeness is on a United States coin worth one _____.

19. Sacagawea joined the Corps of Discovery when Pomp was eight _____ old.

20. Seeing the Pacific _____ was Sacagawea's dream, and she attained it.

Jonas Salk
Developer of the Polio Vaccine

Jonas Salk was born in New York City in 1914, the son of Russian immigrants. His father, Daniel, worked in the garment district, and was ambitious for his children. Two years after Jonas's birth, a terrible poliomyelitis (polio) epidemic hit our East Coast. Polio, caused by a virus, was also called infantile paralysis because it particularly affected young children. This terrifying illness, causing breathing problems, paralysis, crippling, and sometimes death, struck Franklin Delano Roosevelt (FDR) at the age of 39. FDR, although paralyzed, was elected President in 1932. He promoted the March of Dimes to benefit the National Foundation for Infantile Paralysis (NFIP) and fund research. In 1918, there was a worldwide outbreak of another virus, influenza, which killed 22 million people. These tragic events and the NFIP had a big impact on the direction Jonas's life would take.

Born: October 28, 1914, in New York City

Died: June 23, 1995, near San Diego, California

Famous for: developing the first polio vaccine

Jonas's mother, Dora, was a perfectionist. So was Jonas. This is a good trait to have if you're a research scientist, because in science, everything has to be very precise. Extremely confident, Jonas said, "Someday I shall grow up and do something in my own way, without anyone telling me how." He entered college when he was 15. After being introduced to science, he decided to go to medical school. Salk became very interested in research when he learned about different types of vaccines. A vaccine can make someone immune or protected from a particular disease. He chose to work for Dr. Thomas Francis Jr., at the University of Michigan, to develop a vaccine against the influenza virus.

Salk and his work caught the attention of NFIP, which asked him to work on a polio vaccine at the University of Pittsburgh. Salk's colleague Dr. John Enders figured out how to grow the viruses they were experimenting on, which made their work much easier. Once they'd learned how to kill the virus, the doctors injected the resulting vaccine into patients to prevent them from getting polio. (Dr. Albert Sabin developed an oral vaccine, which is also used.) For his life-saving work, which virtually eliminated polio from the globe, Dr. Salk received many awards. In his later life, he worked to develop a vaccine to stop the AIDS virus. At the Salk Institute in La Jolla, California, Salk worked on this project until his death. Now, other scientists continue his fight to eradicate (end) this dreadful disease.

Name _____

DOWN

1. Dora Salk and her son, Jonas, were both _____.

2. _____ stands for the National Foundation for Infantile Paralysis.

4. _____ Franklin Roosevelt got polio when he was 39 years old.

5. President Roosevelt supported the March of _____ to benefit NFIP.

6. The Salk polio _____ protected people from getting the virus.

8. Jonas Salk's parents were immigrants from _____.

10. _____ means an inherited, acquired, or induced protection from a germ.

11. Dr. Salk was _____ years old and still working when he died.

14. Jonas Salk started college when he was _____ years old.

17. When Jonas was young, he dreamed of the day when he wouldn't be _____ what to do.

ACROSS

3. In 1918, _____ killed 22 million people all over the world.

7. _____ was an infectious viral disease that mainly attacked children.

9. Dr. Albert _____ developed an oral polio vaccine, which is also in use.

12. The Salk Institute is in La Jolla, _____.

13. Dr. Salk was working on a vaccine for _____ when he died.

15. At the Salk _____, a vaccine was being developed to prevent AIDS.

16. Polio was also called _____ paralysis.

18. In college, Salk, interested in science, decided to go to _____ school.

19. Polio is caused by a _____, and so is AIDS (acquired immunodeficiency syndrome).

20. Dr. John _____ figured out how to grow viruses in test tubes.

Harriet Tubman
Moses of Her People

There was a sign nailed to a tree that read: WANTED: DEAD OR ALIVE, HARRIET "MOSES" TUBMAN, $12,000 REWARD. Harriet Tubman, born Araminta Ross, was a small but determined woman, who herself had escaped slavery. She also had a deep, ugly scar on her forehead, which she covered up with a scarf or hat. An angry overseer (plantation boss) threw a lead weight at a fleeing slave. On purpose, Harriet got in its way. The resulting injury caused her to have lifelong "sleeping fits," which came on without warning. But this episode tells us why she was known as "the Moses of her people." Like the biblical Moses, she was deeply committed to leading others. That's why her capture was worth $12,000 or more to furious slave owners. They felt (and the law, both North and South, backed them up) that she was "stealing" their property by helping slaves to freedom.

Born: about 1820, on a plantation in Maryland

Died: March 10, 1913, in Auburn, New York

Famous For: leading 300 slaves to freedom on the Underground Railroad

As frightened runaway slaves came out of hiding, they watched Harriet tear the "wanted" poster down. "Are we safe?" they asked out loud. They were, for the time being, but they still had a long way to go on "The Underground Railroad." Harriet Tubman was a "conductor" on this "train," which had no rails or cars. It consisted of carefully planned escape routes northward, to be walked (or run) mostly at night through farms and woods. Sometimes, carts or boats helped. Taking great risks, sympathetic individuals supported the railroad with food, money, and "safe houses," where the fugitives could stop and rest. One time, they even hid in a manure pile, breathing through straws. Harriet wore disguises and had great success fooling her pursuers. It was important that neither she nor any escapees ever get caught. That never happened, so all her secrets remained safe.

Frederick Douglass, himself an escaped slave and famous abolitionist, praised Harriet for willingly taking on so much hardship "to serve our enslaved people." In 1861, during the Civil War, Tubman traveled to South Carolina to work with the Union army as a nurse. Spying for the North, she led a raid on the Combahee River, freeing 750 slaves to fight for the Union. Harriet rescued her parents and brought them to her house (still standing today) in Auburn, New York. Across the street from it, in a home she founded for the sick and elderly, she died at age 93. A bronze tablet honoring Harriet has her own words inscribed on it: "On my Underground Railroad I never ran my train off the track. And I never lost a passenger."

Comprehension-Boosting Crosswords: Famous Americans © 2008 by Sylvia Charlesworth, Scholastic Teaching Resources

Name _____

DOWN

1. Harriet Tubman had a deep _____ on her forehead from being hit with a lead weight.

3. The _____ Railroad had nothing to do with trains.

4. Once, Harriet and a group of fugitives hid in a _____ pile.

6. Harriet was born on a plantation on the eastern shore of _____.

9. During the Civil War, Harriet was a nurse and a _____ for the Union army.

10. Harriet Tubman was sometimes called the _____ of her people.

13. _____ hundred slaves were led to freedom by Harriet Tubman.

14. In Auburn, Harriet established a _____ for the sick and elderly.

16. After she was injured, Harriet Tubman had sleeping _____ for the rest of her life.

ACROSS

1. Many people _____ the Underground Railroad and helped slaves escape.

2. _____, New York, was Harriet's final home.

5. Signs posted about Harriet Tubman read: "Wanted: _____ or Alive."

7. "And I never lost a _____," Harriet said.

8. Harriet's birth name was Araminta _____.

11. A _____ is someone who flees; for example, an escaping slave.

12. Frederick _____ thought Harriet did a lot to help slaves escape.

13. There was a reward offered of twelve _____ dollars for Harriet's capture.

15. On the Combahee River, Tubman freed _____ hundred and fifty slaves.

17. To avoid being captured, Harriet went about in a _____.

18. An _____ had the job of running the plantation and the slaves on it.

George Washington
Father of Our Country

A soldier who knew him said that George Washington was "first in war, first in peace, and first in the hearts of his countrymen." As a young man, Washington fought for the British in the French and Indian War. Virginia was one of the original 13 colonies, and Washington went to defend its western frontier. Well built and more than six feet tall, he was incredibly strong, fiercely courageous, and respected by all who knew him. Out of admiration for him, as both a soldier and a man, an Indian chief and a French general let him go free after they had captured him. When our War of Independence began, George Washington was chosen to lead the Continental Army.

Born: February 22, 1732, in Bridges Creek, Virginia

Died: December 14, 1799, at Mt. Vernon, his estate in Virginia

Famous for: winning our War of Independence; being the first U.S. President

Persistence (never quitting) allowed Washington to win the war he fought from 1775 to 1781. His soldiers were volunteers—they weren't paid, clothed, or even fed regularly. Yet Washington inspired them to keep fighting. He took troops and crossed the freezing Delaware River on Christmas. His surprise attack on a garrison (military post) of soldiers led to victories at Trenton and Princeton (in present-day New Jersey). The general and his men endured the hardships of a winter encampment at Valley Forge, Pennsylvania. Planting false information about his plans, he tricked the enemy into moving its army. Under General Cornwallis, the British surrendered on October 19, 1781. With independence won and his job done, Washington returned to Mt. Vernon and his wife, Martha Custis Washington.

Now there was the peace to consider. Realizing the new country needed a strong basis for its government, Washington fought to have a constitutional convention. Chosen to be its leader, no one worked harder to get the Constitution of the United States ratified (officially approved by the states). Popular as always, Washington was unanimously chosen to be our first President. He took office on April 30, 1789, in New York City. Washington's main job during his two terms in office was to organize the government and figure out how to make our country work.

Washington refused a third term, which set a two-term precedent, (broken only by FDR during World War II). In 1798, when war with France threatened, George Washington, at age 66, was again asked to lead the army. Thankfully, that war never got started. The very next year, while inspecting his Mt. Vernon estate on horseback, he got caught in a drenching rain, took sick, and died (December 14, 1799). The whole nation mourned. George Washington truly was "first in the hearts of his countrymen," as well as the father of his country.

Comprehension-Boosting Crosswords: Famous Americans © 2008 by Sylvia Charlesworth, Scholastic Teaching Resources

Comprehension-Boosting Crosswords
George Washington

DOWN

1. Washington worked hard to get the U.S. Constitution _____.

2. At Valley _____, Washington and his troops suffered hunger and cold.

3. George Washington was born in _____, when it was still a colony.

5. The _____ Army fought the British in our War of Independence.

7. A _____ is a post where troops are housed.

8. The U.S. _____ (Washington, D.C.) is named for George Washington.

10. Washington's estate, Mt. _____, can be visited today.

12. The first _____ of the United States was George Washington.

14. George Washington is called the "_____ of Our Country."

15. Washington was _____ and very courageous.

ACROSS

4. Highly respected, Washington was _____ with friend and foe alike.

6. Washington was sent to defend Virginia's western _____ for the British.

9. General Washington crossed the freezing _____ River on Christmas.

11. Washington was "First in war, first in _____, and first in the hearts of his countrymen."

12. Washington's character trait of _____ led him to success.

13. The _____ of Washington (Pacific Northwest) is named for our first President.

16. The French and _____ War pitted the French against the British.

17. _____ Custis Washington was our first First Lady.

18. A _____ is an act that becomes a model or example.

19. Both Washington and Lincoln were born in the month of _____.

Laura Ingalls Wilder
Chronicler of Pioneer Life

The Homestead Act of 1862 (during the Civil War) had a profound effect on our West, and the family of Laura Ingalls. A popular song, which ended, "Our Uncle Sam is rich enough to give us all a farm!" expressed the jubilation (joy) which greeted the law. Every American over the age of 21 could file papers to claim land (160 acres or ¼ square mile). The acreage had to be plowed and a house built and occupied for five years. Then, after paying a small fee, the homesteader would become the owner of that land. The West, with its wide-open spaces and prairies (rolling grasslands) beckoned to restless Americans. Thousands accepted the offer of land, but the hardships were enormous.

Born: February 7, 1867, near Lake Pepin, Wisconsin

Died: February 10, 1957, on Rocky Ridge Farm in Mansfield, Missouri

Famous for: writing the Little House books, which became a successful TV series

Laura's family endured a variety of misfortunes, including giant hailstones and fires that burned up everything. One summer, grasshoppers ate every bit of their crops. Scarlet fever left Laura's sister Mary blind. Unrelenting cold, near starvation, and poverty caused the Ingalls family (and later Laura and her husband, Almanzo Wilder) to move, seeking better conditions. By 1900, Laura was one of over 600,000 homesteaders. They had claimed 80 million acres of government land. It is their indomitable (not to be defeated) spirit that is the subject matter of Laura's Little House books. She was 63 when she started her series of nine books (*The First Four Years* was published after her death). She lived the pioneer life and wrote about it to amaze, amuse, and enlighten us.

Laura begins her story near Lake Pepin, Wisconsin, in *Little House in the Big Woods.* Next, Charles (Pa) and Caroline (Ma) drove a covered wagon to what turned out to be Osage Indian territory in Kansas, which Laura writes about in *Little House on the Prairie.* "Back-trailing" (going back) to the big woods, the family next moved to a "dug-out" (sod house) near Walnut Grove, Minnesota (*On the Banks of Plum Creek*). After living and working in a hotel in Iowa, the family of six (Laura had three sisters) settled in De Smet in the Dakota Territory (now South Dakota). The books *By the Shores of Silver Lake, The Long Winter, Little Town on the Prairie,* and *These Happy Golden Years* chronicle (tell about) those years. Laura taught school, and then, at age 18, married Almanzo "Manly" Wilder. In the book *Farmer Boy*, she writes about Manly's early life in Malone, New York. Laura and Manly homesteaded in De Smet, but eventually ended up with their daughter, Rose, on Rocky Ridge Farm in the Ozark Mountains. "Running through all the stories is a golden thread," Laura commented. That "thread" was a warm and loving picture of a brave and committed family. Laura was always surprised at her fame and success, but her many happy readers aren't.

Comprehension Boosting Crosswords: Famous Americans © 2008 by Sylvia Charlesworth, Scholastic Teaching Resources

DOWN

1. _____ Territory eventually was divided into North and South Dakota.

3. Laura Ingalls Wilder lived a little past her ninetieth _____.

4. One summer, _____ devoured all the family's crops.

5. The Homestead Act was signed by President Lincoln during the _____ War.

6. Back-_____ meant going back to where you came from.

7. Laura said that her stories had a _____ thread running through them.

14. A homestead claim had 160 _____ or ¼ of a square mile.

17. The Little House books later became a _____ series.

ACROSS

2. Uncle _____ is a nickname for the United States of America.

6. By mistake, the Ingalls family ended up in Osage Indian _____.

8. The _____ Act of 1862 changed the American West.

9. Laura's nickname for her husband, Almanzo Wilder, was _____.

10. Laura's sister Mary had scarlet fever, which left her _____.

11. A _____ house (also called a dug-out) was a mud cave topped with grass.

12. Laura and Manly's last home was in the _____ Mountains of Missouri.

13. Almanzo Wilder spent his boyhood in _____, New York.

15. A _____ is a large area of rolling grassland.

16. The Ingalls family finally settled down in _____ (in present-day South Dakota).

18. Laura Ingalls Wilder was past the age of _____ when she started writing her books.

19. There are nine Little _____ books; one was published after Laura died.

The Wright Brothers
Pioneers of the Airplane

"We could hardly wait for morning to come to get at something that interested us. *That's* happiness," said Orville Wright. He and his brother Wilbur were interested in many things, but they both were consumed with a passion to fly. They were so close, many people thought they were twins, but they didn't look alike, and they had different personalities. Wilbur was a quiet dreamer, but Orville was outgoing and liked to dress impeccably (perfectly). Their father, Milton, declared them "equal in their inventions" and always supported their endeavors. He is credited with igniting their interest in flying, when he brought them a toy helicopter made of bamboo, paper, cork, and twisted rubber bands. Their mother, Susan, who liked working with her hands, passed on her mechanical aptitude (ability) to her sons. The brothers started out as successful printers. Then bicycling became a big craze, so they decided to go into the bicycle business, first repairing and then modifying them. Their bicycle business made them wealthy and worked well for them. In Dayton, Ohio, where they lived, the winters were cold, and the bicycle business dropped off. That meant they could spend time on their flying experiments.

> **Born:** Wilbur, April 16, 1867 (Millville, IN); Orville, August 19, 1871 (Dayton, OH)
>
> **Died:** Wilbur, May 30, 1912, in Dayton; Orville, January 30, 1948, in Dayton
>
> **Famous for:** making the first successful engine-powered, man-carrying flight

From the beginning of time, people have wanted to fly. In the early 1500s, Leonardo da Vinci drew designs for flying machines. The early aviation pioneers began with gliders, sometimes looking like giant insects riding the breeze. It was the Wright Brothers who solved the mechanical challenges that enabled airplanes to have controlled flight. Their discoveries are still in use in aviation today. They came up with a successful wing design. They realized wings had to tilt up and down like the wings on the buzzards they watched flying. In the middle of the night, Orville figured out the rudder at the back of their craft had to move. They needed to design a lightweight engine, a way to steer, and a way to land.

They also needed courage and the right place to test their inventions. They had the courage, and the right place turned out to be Kitty Hawk, on the Outer Banks of North Carolina. There was often a forceful wind on Kill Devil Hills, and tons of sand to provide a safe landing. On December 17, 1903, Orville piloted that first historic flight. It lasted only 12 seconds, but it was revolutionary. When Neil Armstrong stepped on the moon, he carried a piece of the material from the wing of that plane, now called the *Kitty Hawk*. Wilbur and Orville Wright started the Age of Flight. It was more than a hundred years ago, and nothing has been the same since!

Comprehension-Boosting Crosswords: Famous Americans © 2008 by Sylvia Charlesworth, Scholastic Teaching Resources

Name _____

DOWN

2. The Wright Brothers inherited their mechanical ability from their _____.

3. The boys' father gave them a toy _____ and started their interest in flying.

4. Early attempts to fly began with _____.

5. Wilbur and Orville watched _____ fly to learn flying techniques.

6. The Wright Brothers lived in _____, Ohio, most of their lives.

7. Orville said that doing what interested him was _____.

8. The strong winds on Kill _____ Hills helped the first plane to fly.

12. Success in the _____ business enabled the Wright Brothers to pursue their flying experiments.

14. The first business the brothers worked in was _____.

ACROSS

1. The Wright Brothers' historic first flight was _____ 17, 1903.

9. *Kitty* _____ is now the name of the Wright Brothers' first airplane.

10. The town of Kitty Hawk is in North _____.

11. It was very important to have a lightweight _____.

13. They discovered the wings of their airplane needed to _____ like a bird's.

15. _____ was more outgoing than his brother.

16. The _____ on the back of the airplane needed to move on demand.

17. Kitty Hawk and Kill Devil Hills are on the Outer _____ of North Carolina.

18. _____ was quiet and a bit of a dreamer.

19. The first flight lasted twelve _____.

20. Neil _____ took a piece of the cotton wing of the *Kitty Hawk* to the moon.

Answer Key

SUSAN B. ANTHONY
(page 8)

Down:
1. teacher
3. suffrage
6. arrested
7. Stanton
8. voting
9. Rochester
10. money
11. fine
14. rights

Across:
2. Quaker
4. failure
5. Falls
7. support
12. abolitionists
13. Historic
15. nineteenth
16. fifty
17. husband
18. Lucretia
19. Massachusetts

NEIL ARMSTRONG
(page 10)

Down:
1. Korean
4. Apollo
5. lunar
6. decade
9. Kennedy
10. mankind
13. *Eagle*
14. rocket
15. bakery

Across:
2. orbit
3. astronaut
7. *Gemini*
8. docking
11. NASA
12. Canaveral
16. Wapakoneta
17. aeronautical
18. Aldrin
19. sixteenth
20. days

GEORGE WASHINGTON CARVER
(page 12)

Down:
1. Booker
2. Ford
3. Carter
4. Simpson
5. agriculture
6. peanuts
8. schools
11. growing
12. king
13. lapel
14. Carver
15. Civil
18. Ames

Across:
6. potatoes
7. Congress
9. Mariah
10. Tuskegee
16. slave
17. painting
19. flowers

ROBERTO CLEMENTE
(page 14)

Down:
2. autobiography
3. guava
5. Montreal
6. Buccaneers
9. Giants
11. League
15. *Barrio*
18. cane
20. old

Across:
1. Carolina
4. Puerto
7. Managua
8. pitch
10. rags
12. natural
13. Baseball
14. Juan
16. Mays
17. Hispanic
19. Dodgers

DAVY CROCKETT
(page 16)

Down:
1. Davy
2. Betsy
4. Alamo
5. frontier
6. alligator
7. Creek
8. Jackson
9. trial
10. Congress
14. peace

Across:
3. Anna
6. Antonio
11. coonskin
12. education
13. Legislature
15. old
16. series
17. TN
18. Texas
19. wildcats

FREDERICK DOUGLASS
(page 18)

Down:
1. Anna
2. Maryland
3. extemporaneous
5. Augustus
6. dawn
9. Sunday
11. Sophia
12. Lincoln
14. Douglass
17. women

Across:
3. education
4. autobiography
7. Star
8. grandparents
10. abolitionists
13. illegal
15. uniform
16. caulk
18. monument
19. Rochester

AMELIA EARHART
(page 20)

Down:
1. Columbia
3. Japanese
4. Noonan
6. grandparents
7. Howland
8. Pacific
11. Electra
12. miles
13. New
15. Kansas

Across:
2. freedom
5. autogiro
9. gasoline
10. Atlantic
12. Meely
14. world
16. cutter
17. passenger
18. social
19. *Itasca*

THOMAS ALVA EDISON
(page 22)

Down:
1. perspiration
2. layover
3. mother
6. butcher
7. patents
8. telephone
11. days
14. research
18. wizard

Across:
4. vegetables
5. work
9. phonograph
10. Menlo
12. telegrapher
13. newspaper
15. son
16. four
17. Ohio
19. incandescent
20. Orange

BENJAMIN FRANKLIN
(page 24)

Down:
1. Boston
2. adage
3. copper
5. electricity
6. printing
7. minister
8. seventeen
10. France
13. stove
14. *Almanack*
16. money

Across:
1. Birthday
4. postmaster
9. Independence
11. University
12. penny
15. slavery
17. odometer
18. England
19. bifocals

Answer Key

THOMAS JEFFERSON
(page 26)

Down:
1. obelisk
3. Monticello
4. writer
5. slavery
7. British
8. Napoleon
9. Adams
12. unalienable
14. confidence
15. Clark
16. collection

Across:
2. religious
6. Louisiana
10. architecture
11. education
13. democracy
17. Virginia
18. Declaration
19. million
20. Congress

HELEN KELLER
(page 28)

Down:
1. manual
2. Little
3. Sullivan
6. deaf
7. poorhouse
8. Dickens
14. *Worker*
16. pantry

Across:
4. versa
5. Radcliffe
7. pump
9. Tuscumbia
10. travel
11. old
12. miracles
13. Bell
15. pantomime
17. author
18. nineteen
19. Connecticut

DR. MARTIN LUTHER KING, JR.
(page 30)

Down:
1. Dream
3. Birmingham
5. jail
8. Center
9. orator
11. Promised
12. violent
13. American

Across:
2. Nobel
4. Lorraine
6. Coretta
7. cadence
10. Lincoln
14. thirty
15. segregation
16. consciences
17. civil
18. freedom
19. Atlanta
20. holiday

MERIWETHER LEWIS & WILLIAM CLARK
(page 32)

Down:
1. Jefferson
3. appendicitis
4. Louisiana
6. anniversary
9. Pomp
11. Sacagawea
13. ocean
16. army
19. Louis

Across:
2. Clark
5. Mackenzie
7. Oregon
8. Expedition
10. years
12. Meriwether
14. of
15. Captain
17. fauna
18. grizzly
20. flora

ABRAHAM LINCOLN
(page 34)

Down:
1. lawyer
2. emancipate
3. Mary
5. ax
6. Springfield
7. Civil
8. Douglas
11. Union
14. theater

16. Booth

Across:
1. Lee
4. Abraham
9. Kentucky
10. humor
12. Mississippi
13. Gettysburg
15. malice
17. Amendment
18. Memorial
19. Sumter

THURGOOD MARSHALL
(page 36)

Down:
1. years
2. balcony
4. fists
6. Lyndon
9. Thoroughgood
11. separate
13. Lincoln
16. Kennedy
18. Olive

Across:
3. General
5. Civil
7. cases
8. Constitution
10. desegregation
12. justice
14. fighters
15. Howard
17. Baltimore
19. Education
20. NAACP

JOHN MUIR
(page 38)

Down:
1. strict
2. beauty
4. mountains
7. Scotland
9. inventor
10. Alaska
13. Sierra
15. Rainier

Across:
3. writer
5. Francisco
6. blind
8. creation
11. Yosemite
12. trek
13. Sequoia
14. beard
16. Wisconsin
17. glaciers
18. Angeles
19. daughters

ROSA PARKS
(page 40)

Down:
1. John
2. December
5. segregation
7. plaintiff
10. guilty
12. Tuskegee
13. Martin
16. Story
17. NAACP

Across:
3. boycott
4. Congressional
6. Montgomery
8. Dearborn
9. driver
11. Washington
14. third
15. tired
16. Smithsonian
18. seamstress
19. protests

ELEANOR ROOSEVELT
(page 42)

Down:
1. Kennedy
2. Truman
4. polio
5. World
6. Theodore
10. Depression
12. conscience
14. Universal
16. England

Across:
3. Eleanor
7. orphan
8. beautiful
9. FDR
11. compassionate
13. humanitarian
15. charity
17. five
18. United
19. Granny
20. Sara

Answer Key

THEODORE ROOSEVELT
(page 44)

Down:
1. Panama
3. Alice
5. reptiles
7. conservationist
10. cavalry
12. asthma
14. Nobel
16. Oyster
17. food

Across:
2. Harvard
4. law
6. McKinley
8. Badlands
9. sixty
11. Dakota
13. Western
15. tornado
18. five
19. teddy
20. Riders

SACAGAWEA
(page 46)

Down:
2. Bird
3. Shoshone
4. journals
6. Cameahwait
7. horses
9. states
11. buffalo
12. capsize
14. edible
16. Mandan

Across:
1. cradleboard
5. nomadic
8. Pomp
10. Charbonneau
13. dates
15. tepees
17. Hidatsa
18. dollar
19. weeks
20. Ocean

DR. JONAS SALK
(page 48)

Down:
1. perfectionists
2. NFIP
4. President
5. Dimes
6. vaccine
8. Russia
10. immunity
11. eighty
14. fifteen
17. told

Across:
3. influenza
7. poliomyelitis
9. Sabin
12. California
13. AIDS
15. Institute
16. infantile
18. medical
19. virus
20. Enders

HARRIET TUBMAN
(page 50)

Down:
1. scar
3. Underground
4. manure
6. Maryland
9. spy
10. Moses
13. three
14. home
16. fits

Across:
1. supported
2. Auburn
5. Dead
7. passenger
8. Ross
11. fugitive
12. Douglass
13. thousand
15. seven
17. disguise
18. overseer

GEORGE WASHINGTON
(page 52)

Down:
1. ratified
2. Forge
3. Virginia
5. Continental
7. garrison
8. capital
10. Vernon
12. President
14. Father
15. strong

Across:
4. popular
6. frontier
9. Delaware
11. peace
12. persistence
13. state
16. Indian
17. Martha
18. precedent
19. February

LAURA INGALLS WILDER
(page 54)

Down:
1. Dakota
3. birthday
4. grasshoppers
5. Civil
6. trailing
7. golden
14. acres
17. TV

Across:
2. Sam
6. Territory
8. Homestead
9. Manly
10. blind
11. sod
12. Ozark
13. Malone
15. prairie
16. De Smet
18. sixty
19. House

THE WRIGHT BROTHERS
(page 56)

Down:
2. mother
3. helicopter
4. gliders
5. buzzards
6. Dayton
7. happiness
8. Devil
12. bicycle
14. printing

Across:
1. December
9. *Hawk*
10. Carolina
11. engine
13. tilt
15. Orville
16. rudder
17. Banks
18. Wilbur
19. seconds
20. Armstrong

Notes